Thinking Visually

*Step-by-step exercises that promote visual, auditory
and kinesthetic learning*

OLIVER CAVIGLIOLI

IAN HARRIS

Pembroke Publishers Limited

© 2003 Oliver Caviglioli and Ian Harris
Pembroke Publishers
538 Hood Road
Markham, Ontario, Canada L3R 3K9
www.pembrokepublishers.com

Distributed in the U.S. by Stenhouse Publishers
477 Congress Street
Portland, ME 04101
www.stenhouse.com

All rights reserved.
No part of this publication may be reproduced in any form or by any means electronic or mechanical, including photocopy, recording, or any information, storage or retrieval system, without permission in writing from the publisher.

This edition is adapted from a book originally published in the U.K. by Network Educational Press Ltd., P.O. Box 635, Stafford, ST16 1BF.

Every effort has been made to contact copyright holders for permission to reproduce borrowed material. The publishers apologize for any omissions and will be pleased to rectify them in subsequent reprints of the book.

We acknowledge the financial support of the Government of Canada through the Book Publishing Industry Development Program (BPIDP) for our publishing activities.

We acknowledge the Government of Ontario through the Ontario Media Development Corporation's Ontario Book Initiative.

National Library of Canada Cataloguing in Publication

Caviglioli, Oliver
    Thinking visually : step-by-step exercises that promote visual, auditory and kinesthetic learning / Oliver Caviglioli, Ian Harris, Graham Foster. -- Canadian ed.

Previous ed. published 2000 under title: Mapwise.
Includes bibliographical references and index.
For use in grades K-6.
ISBN 1-55138-155-9

1. Visual learning. 2. Auditory perception in children. 3. Movement education. I. Harris, Ian II. Foster, Graham III. Title. IV. Title: Mapwise.

LB1067.5.C39 2003370.15'23C2003-902741-4

Editor: Carol-Ann Freeman, Gina Walker
Layout & design: Neil Hawkins, Jay Tee Graphics Ltd.
Illustrations: Oliver Caviglioli
Cover Design: John Zehethofer
Cover Photo: Photo Disk

Printed and bound in Canada
9 8 7 6 5 4 3 2 1

Contents

Foreword

Students learn better when they are able to articulate their thought and learning processes when completing a task. While this is particularly true for struggling learners, gifted students also recognize the benefit of being explicit about their thinking when they confront challenging learning tasks. *Thinking Visually* is a companion to other professional resources that focus on the value of helping students learn how to learn.

Thinking Visually promotes the power of mapping for thinking and learning. While other resources offer collections of graphic organizers, *Thinking Visually* provides step-by-step guides for mapping ideas, subjects, projects and concepts. It argues that mapping is most effectively learned in the context of ongoing subject study. While other sources on strategic learning stress the value of articulating one's approach before, during and after completing a task, *Thinking Visually* facilitates a visual articulation of one's approach throughout the learning process. *Thinking Visually* amplifies the message that teachers should model strategies.

Thinking Visually is solidly rooted in learning theory – particularly the insight that new learning needs to fit into existing familiar structures or mental models. Mapping is a useful strategy for expressing one's current understanding of a topic and for noting one's developing understanding. Therefore, *Thinking Visually* complements professional resources which advocate a demystifying of the learning process and let students in on the secrets of learning.

Other resources on thinking skills and strategies such as *I Think, Therefore I Learn*, recognize that thinking and learning are enhanced when students reflect on their learning tasks, consider alternatives, figure out what works best for them and set goals for future learning. Visual learning strategies, especially mapping, are useful and motivational options for wide-ranging learning tasks. Current resources on thinking and learning unrelentingly emphasize the importance of students articulating how they go about completing tasks; *Thinking Visually* amplifies this emphasis.

Teachers interested in differentiated instruction will value the book's attention to how mapping benefits visual, auditory and kinesthetic learners. *Thinking Visually* also looks at how mapping can be used to develop thinking skills emphasized in current curriculum documents. Samples of student and teacher maps will certainly be useful for examples and models in the classroom.

Thinking Visually is a valuable reference for teachers and anyone else committed to student ownership and responsibility for their own learning.

Graham Foster
author of *I Think, Therefore I Learn*

Introduction

the inside story

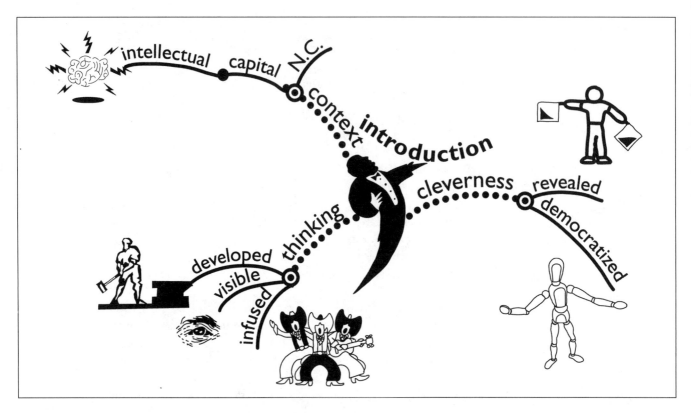

"Learning is about searching out meaning and imposing structure ... It equips students to go beyond the information given, to deal systematically yet flexibly with novel problems and situations, to adopt a critical attitude to information and argument, as well as to communicate effectively ... If students are to become better thinkers – to learn meaningfully, to think flexibly and to make reasoned judgments – then they must be taught explicitly how to do it."

Through mapping, students become better thinkers and learners. Mapping ensures that tasks will always "have a degree of open-endedness and uncertainty to permit learners to impose meaning or to make judgments or to produce multiple solutions". Mapping enables learners "to make their own thought processes more explicit"; it ensures that "talking about thinking – questioning, predicting, contradicting, doubting – is not only tolerated but actively pursued".

Thinking Visually describes a technique with several names: model mapping, mind mapping, memory mapping, semantic mapping, thought-webbing and sometimes just mapping or webbing. The mapping technique challenges students to comprehend meaning and to impose structure as they learn. It helps students develop and consolidate concepts and to learn new vocabulary. Throughout this book, this technique will be referred to as "mapping".

Using mapping, you are able to produce models of your thoughts about a particular concept or idea – hence the name "mapping". *Thinking Visually* shows how mapping can be used as a powerful learning technique available to both teachers and learners. *Thinking Visually* will emphasize how mapping can be used to

- teach thinking skills as part of subject delivery
- improve reading and writing skills
- support each stage of the learning process
- demonstrate and develop intelligence
- develop four essential learning skills that all learners need – irrespective of their preferred learning style
- transform the teaching and learning systems in operation in classrooms.

Ultimately *Thinking Visually* will support you in helping your students to understand themselves and the world around them, both at school and beyond. *Thinking Visually* is intended to increase both your own and your students' capacity for learning.

Learning how to learn

It is interesting to note, that while teachers *are* now focusing on the "process of learning", this term has not emphasized models of, or strategies for, the actual processes of thinking and learning that occur within the learner's mind. Schools have learned how to design visually stimulating environments, how to create safe and challenging cultures, how to foster self-esteem, how to deliver material in multi-sensory ways and in a brain-friendly sequence, how to engage the learner's memory, how to meet the learner's physiological needs and even how to integrate ambient music into learning. All these strategies are a tremendous boost to the learner and make learning more likely to happen. But these strategies do not tell us what learning actually *is* or how it occurs. They therefore comprise only part of what is involved in the well-worn phrase "learning how to learn".

In short, it is currently not strictly accurate to say that effective instruction is about "learning how to learn". A more accurate description might be "learning how to make learning more likely". When asked what they mean by "learning how to learn", colleagues' answers relate to the conditions of learning.

How much better would results be if learners, in addition to experiencing stimulating environments and positive personal states, also had a tool that gave them access to the very structure of their thinking and learning? What if all learners had a technique that could be used to develop their thinking skills? What if all learners knew how to generate ideas, organize concepts, ensure recall and model the thinking of subject specialists? And what if this tool was fun to use, very individualized and easily communicable? Furthermore, what if it was of equal benefit to teachers in their planning, teaching and assessment of students' understanding?

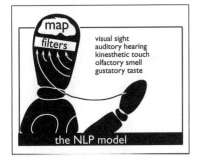

map
filters

visual sight
auditory hearing
kinesthetic touch
olfactory smell
gustatory taste

the NLP model

Neuro Linguistic Programming

The authors are not alone in their passion for modelling the origins of excellence; the very basis of NLP (Neuro Linguistic Programming) is predicated on this intention. In her book on NLP and learning, Dianne Beaver looks at modelling successful learners. She goes about this by modelling what she can see — behavior. Much to her consternation, the best students in the class

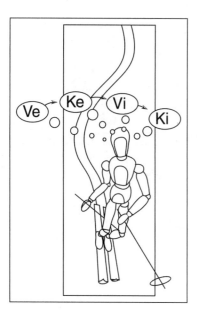

exhibited the worst physical states for learning. They slouched, breathed shallowly, frowned, and worried over their work! This failure is instructive. It shows the limits of lower order analysis.

By contrast, Anthony Robbins, an extraordinarily successful NLP practitioner, has looked at modelling learning from the inside. Through extremely detailed questioning of people who have mastered various activities, Robbins was able to come up with what he calls "the syntax of success". In modelling an expert skier, for example, Robbins found the exact sequence of internal sensory action he needed to go through. It consisted of very precise directions for attention, such as switching from visual external (watching the expert skier) and kinesthetic external (moving your body as the expert skier is moving), to visual internal (creating an internal picture of the expert skier) and then to kinesthetic internal (feeling the sensation of moving without actually moving).

The sequence continues, but this much gives a sense of the possibility of entering into the same mental landscape as those you are modelling. It is this ability to access internal terrains that gives model mapping such potential for transformation learning. What is going on in the terrain that we call our mind? How can we see the "inside story"?

Compelling reasons

The emphasis of this book is to show how mapping can "democratize" cleverness by literally showing us what it looks like. It can externalize the internal and organized thinking of clever people, which is the basis for their effective decisions and actions. If thinking is spread out onto a map, understanding can be both communicated and developed. Translating rapid, private, ephemeral and abstract thinking into static, public, concrete and accessible demonstrations reveals concepts to all learners.

Essentially, then, mapping supports teachers' explanations and learners' understanding. The qualities of mapping that are brought to the fore in *Thinking Visually*, in addition to the established benefits of left-right brain laterality promoted by Tony Buzan, should make mapping irresistible to schools.

Teachers enhance learning by helping students recognize the connection between skills and strategies. In this book skills refer to WHAT students do to complete a learning task. Bloom's taxonomy is a familiar hierarchy of thinking skills including knowledge, comprehension, application, analysis, synthesis and evaluation. Strategies refer to KNOW-HOW students employ to complete a learning task. Mapping is a powerful strategy that relates to a wide range of thinking skills. Through mapping, students summarize and synthesize knowledge as part of learning tasks that require application, analysis and evaluation.

Thinking Visually aims to provoke you to consider why you are not yet providing this invaluable tool to your students. By completing the step-by-step instructions, you will become accomplished in creating maps. By integrating maps into your teaching, you and your students will benefit. Quite simply, you will be expanding your students' capacity for learning and thinking.

1 Maps

charting their history, value, function, design and applications

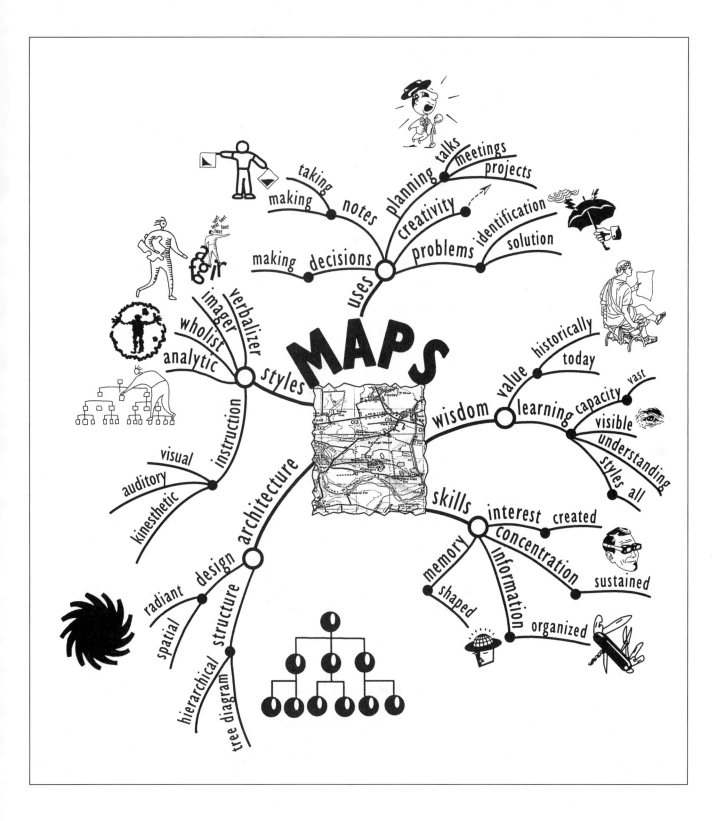

The standard forms of communications we use can be seen as maps. They enable us to get beyond our own ideas to those of others. They enable us to find new information. We trade our perceptions and ideas through the currency of maps … A map is anything that shows you the way from one point to another, from one level of understanding to another.

Richard Saul Wurman

The BBC television series *Blackadder Goes Forth* is set during the First World War. In one episode, General Melchett asks his aid, Captain Darling, for a map of the Western Front: "At ease everybody. Now, where's my map? Come on."

Darling hands Melchett the map, who opens it up on the desk. Melchett comments to Darling, "It's a barren featureless desert out there, isn't it", to which Darling responds, "It's the other side sir".

Maps are – if you know how to use them – very useful. Had General Melchett had access to *Thinking Visually*, this chapter would have helped him get the most out of using maps.

This chapter is divided up into the following sections.

- The wisdom of maps
- Information architecture
- Brain-compatible learning
- Benefits of mapping
- Note-making and note-taking
- Use it or lose it

The wisdom of maps

Maps are not a recent invention. They have a history of centuries and – as the cave paintings of early humans and the hieroglyphics of ancient Egypt illustrate – visual note-taking has been around for even longer.

The use and availability of maps have played a crucial part in the unfolding of history. As the Europeans took over North America, maps were used to carve up the Indian Territories; the Treaty of Versailles saw Europe literally redrawn; and again following the Second World War, Europe was divided between East and West. Throughout history, in fact, maps have always been equated with power, whether they depicted hunting grounds, military sites, trade routes or buried treasure. Maps had value and were prized.

In another episode of *Blackadder Goes Forth*, Lieutenant George and Captain Blackadder are sent on a night patrol to draw the German trenches. As they are crawling around in the mud Captain Blackadder asks Lieutenant George, "Where the hell are we?"

> **George** (looking at the map)**:** Well it's a bit difficult to say. We appear to have crawled into an area marked with mushrooms.
> **Blackadder:** What do those symbols denote?
> **George:** That we are in a field of mushrooms?
> **Blackadder:** Lieutenant – that is a military map. It is unlikely to list interesting flora and fungi. Look at the key and you'll discover that those mushrooms aren't for picking.
> **George:** Good Lord you're quite right, Sir. It says "mine". So, these mushrooms must belong to the man who made the map!

[Maps] can make sense of chaos, define the abstract with the concrete, and generally act as weapons by which we can subdue complex ideas and unruly numbers. Well-crafted maps can reduce anxiety.

Richard Saul Wurman

We can draw several useful lessons from this. First, the ability to read and understand maps can be an enriching (and in Lieutenant George's case life-saving) experience. Second, maps show an individual's, a group's or an organization's mental *representation* of an area of territory – they are *not*, however, the territory itself. The fact that Melchett did not realize that he was looking at the wrong side of the map suggests, perhaps, how unfamiliar the

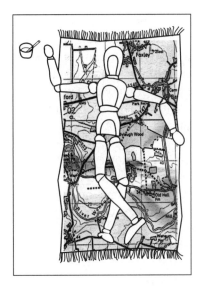

generals were with the reality of warfare in the trenches. These two examples serve to illustrate the usefulness of being able to read and understand maps.

Today it is unlikely that we will be using maps to look for buried treasure, follow trade routes or manoeuvre around hunting grounds. But maps continue to reveal treasures. Contemporary treasures may be less dramatic and often more abstract, but they remain things that we value. We now live in an age centred on knowledge; information is the backdrop for, and the very substance of, many of our endeavors. The treasure we seek is *knowledge* and the subsequent meaning we can create from it.

Maps can play a crucial part in finding our treasure – revealing knowledge and encouraging confidence. It is just unfortunate, perhaps, that our contemporary treasure is not perceived as being as glamorous as buried bullion.

Some people doubt that any topic can be mapped. What of the arts, for example? Surely there are some areas that are too subtle to be the subject of this cartographic analysis. Well, there can be no more subtle area than that of human consciousness and this has been successfully "mapped".

The constraints of linear presentation

Linear orientation of information dominates our lives, because we read and write in lines of text that – in western cultures – we follow from left-to-right. Let us consider what we do with the information that we read in this left-to-right fashion. As we finish one page and turn to the next, we have to store the essential information of the first page in our memory. Of course, we are not conscious that we do this but if we did not the next page would be meaningless since it would have nothing to link with or hook in to. Furthermore, we do not store the information in a linear sequence, since each new piece of information in a book does not necessarily refer to the piece immediately preceding it. Instead, the reader is constantly asked to link new information to old information that may have been read several pages before.

So, we take information from linear text and process it in a non-linear way. It is not, perhaps, surprising that a significant number of people have difficulty doing this, given the complexity of the task.

The reading example illustrates that we do not think in a linear way. This means that, since the development of writing, humans have had to impose upon themselves a continual behavior modification programme in order to process information provided as text. Our behavior has been shaped by the linear, left-to-right orientation of written text, and rewards have gone to those who master this format. Maps have played a much smaller part in our communication systems despite their ability to clarify and reveal concepts.

By presenting information outside of the constraints of a linear mode, maps offer the reader not just the information depicted in each section of the map, but also the relationships between the sections. The total knowledge gained exemplifies the notion that the whole is more than the sum of its parts.

Wurman makes an analogy in contrasting a plane journey that follows a straight line (digital), with a pedestrian journey that involves, by necessity, a more circuitous route (analogue). Getting lost is always a possibility with the "analogue" walk, though with a map you can see how to get back on course. A "digital" plane journey more-or-less guarantees your arrival at the destination – as long as you don't fall out!

Most people have a fairly limited concept of a map as a depiction of a particular geographic location. To find our way through information, we also rely on maps that will tell us where we are in relation to the information, give us a sense of perspective, and enable us to make comparisons between information.

Richard Saul Wurman

Maps are the metaphoric means by which we can understand and act upon information from outside sources. A map by definition must perform, whether it is a multimillion dollar, four-color production of the national weather system or two cans of beer on a counter showing the relationship of a friend's new house to his old one.

Richard Saul Wurman

Trying to wade through information without a sense of structure is like going to the Library of Congress and aimlessly combing the shelves for a particular book. Once you have a sense of how the whole is organized, you will reduce the frustration of searching for a needle in a haystack. Even if the needle is all that you need, it will behove you to know how the hay is organized.

Richard Saul Wurman

We don't "see" with our eyes at all, but we see with our brain.

Harry Alder and *Beryl Heather*

As Lieutenant George and General Melchett illustrate beautifully, reading maps requires some degree of training, otherwise the wealth of information within them can confuse rather than simplify. You can get lost. Initially it may seem strange that any training is needed as "… many users [of maps] would maintain that using a map should require no more than normal vision and average intelligence". However, compared to the number of years spent in educating students to use linear means of communicating, the proposition of teaching them to read maps seems reasonable.

Readers of maps need to understand how the map is constructed. The very nature of the construction gives meaning to the content. Different types of maps have different methods of organization. The organization of some types is more evident than that of others. Later in the book, in chapter 2, the organizing principles of model maps will be explained. We look now at an aspect of maps that distinguishes them from text – images.

Using images

We have a need to look for patterns. Schools do not abandon visual learning entirely – they simply do not spend much time teaching it. If you reflect on the fact that "The way we learn, and subsequently remember, bears a strong relationship to the way our senses operate", it becomes clear that "we, as educators, cannot afford to ignore the fact that a very high proportion of all sensory learning is visual". The design and use of visual learning techniques, and opportunities for their use, should carry a higher priority in education and would benefit from extended research. Alistair Smith and Nicola Call argue strongly to reconsider the current lack of emphasis placed on visual learning:

"Perhaps our natural disposition towards organizing information in our heads through visual patterns and spatial relationships is undervalued. In arguing for the teaching and the use of mapping techniques we are arguing for the extension of the visual and spatial propensity that seems an inherent part of our neural architecture. We are all mappers."

Our capacity for visual recall is astonishing. Recently, Ian recovered a store of his old comics that had been in his father's attic for over 20 years. This is how he described looking at them again. "I was acutely aware, as I went from one front cover to the next, that none of them surprised me. I went through over a thousand comics and each and every one was familiar to me. As I read through a few comic strips it was the pictures not the words that took me back to my childhood. On one front cover of a 'Tiger and Scorcher' comic Billy Dane was playing cricket … and his cricket bat, because of the angle it was drawn at, seemed shorter than a real bat. This picture took me back to the chair by the stove in my Grandparents' house where I had been when I first read the story. Without thinking I recalled what my Grandmother was cooking at the time – I could smell the stew and dumplings – where my Grandad had been that morning and my confusion at why the artist had drawn such a short bat."

How many times have you heard people say "I never forget a face"? When you bump into an old acquaintance or ex-colleague, what do you remember first – the face or the name? The experiments of Haber in the early 1970s revealed that we have a nearly perfect recall of images. Eventually viewing over 2500 images at a rate of one per second, participants in Haber's visual experiment achieved an accuracy of recall of between 85% and 95%.

Images provide such strong, stimulating and memorable hooks for memory. We readily internalize images, and are able to recall minor details within them. This "… capacity to internalize and manipulate visual images is a powerful one which some researchers have gone on to link to a stage in our evolutionary development. The ability to locate and move from a source of threat, or to visually map the position of traps, or to direct oneself back to a herd of migrating beasts would help our ancestors survive". It is no surprise, then, that images have continued to be an inherent part of maps.

Information architecture

When maps are deconstructed, we can see that they have essentially the same structure as a traditional tree diagram used to represent anything from the classification of animals to the management of a business.

While the graphic layout of a tree diagram may appear to be far removed from a map, it contains exactly the same organizing principles of construction. The main difference is that in a tree diagram, the most significant concept is found at the top with those lower down represented in descending order of importance. In maps the most important concept is at the centre, with the subordinate concepts radiating to the edges. The two illustrations that follow, for example, show the same information – at the top of the next page it is shown as a tree diagram (on its side in this case) while below it is shown as a map.

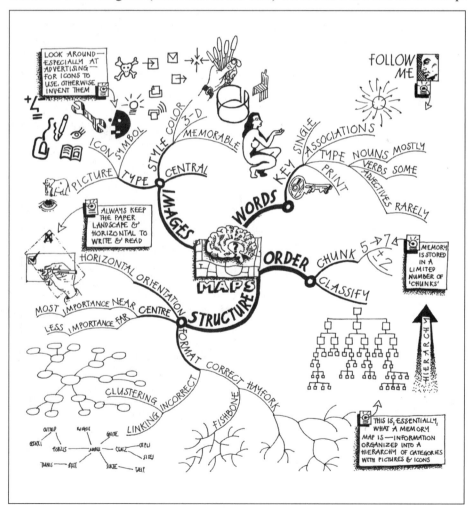

13

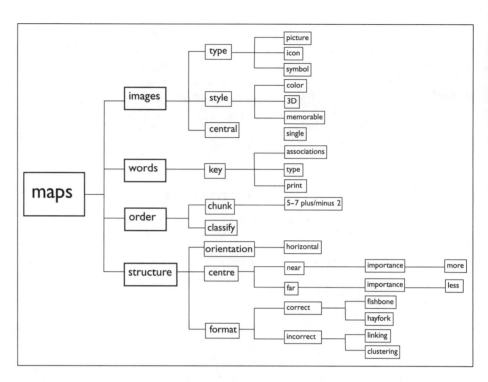

In order to see that these two formats are essentially the same, imagine a tree diagram drawn on paper, with the central concept at the top and the subordinate branches cascading down below it. Now imagine cutting the main subordinate branches off from the main concept, and then cutting between them to separate them. Now you could arrange these subordinate branches around the main concept, instead of below it, and essentially create a map. The main ideas would be in the centre and the lesser concepts would radiate towards the edge. The illustration below shows a tree diagram chopped up and spread around the main concept – you can see that it is effectively the same as the map on page 9.

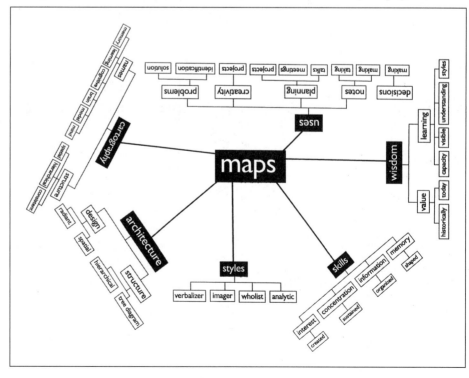

Thought maps, like all maps, share this basic organizing structure. They may be presented as "holographic mind projections", likened to the synapses of the brain, described as "organic thought generators", and so on, but they are fundamentally the same as the classification diagrams used by the Victorians in their quest to analyze and explain the world. The rules and conventions of mapping should not disguise or confuse this fact.

What maps have in contrast to formal tree diagrams is design. This is not to say that they are necessarily artistic in nature. Anybody can construct a map with the inclusion of images – fine art training is not a requirement. Nor is the belief that you are not a visual learner any sort of real impediment.

Seen from the perspective of design, a map very largely follows its basic principles of arrangement, balance, color, dynamism, emphasis, fidelity and graphic harmony. Even if that list seems rather daunting, you can see that maps have the following characteristics, which are totally lacking from linear notes: "visual rhythm, visual pattern, color image, visualization, dimension, spatial awareness, gestalt (wholeness), association".

As maps are visual, it is inevitable that some design or artistic perspective is attributed to them. It is not primarily an artistic distinction that determines their construction, however. It is a balance between the organizational nature of the topic to be mapped and the creativity in finding a spatial structure to represent the conceptual interpretation the mapper has of the topic. Chapter 2 explains exactly what this entails; it is mentioned here simply to emphasize that structures of maps cannot be predetermined. Individuality molds the nature of the topic under focus. That is why it is not appropriate to offer students a bare map with only the branches drawn, as has been suggested elsewhere.

Maps are models of our thoughts, and so they differ from individual to individual. They represent the way in which our thoughts inter-relate. This matrix of concepts constitutes the meanings we have made of our world. We bring together all our sense impressions and thoughts in this creation, that we can call a schema. "Schema" is the technical term used by psychologists to describe the construction of our understanding. Chapter 7 examines in detail the development of schemas; here we focus on the fact that the raw data for our schemas come from our total experience of our environment. Because of this, we know that both sides of our brain have been involved.

Brain-compatible learning

Much has been written about hemispheric learning – how the left and right brain operate. Indeed, much use of this is made to justify the use of maps. However, Robert Ornstein, winner of the Nobel prize for his discovery of left–right brain differences, comments that the over-simplified way in which his research is interpreted by non-scientists concerns him. Similarly, implying that the connections made on a map are analogous to the synaptic connections in the brain is not strictly appropriate.

There does, however, seem to be agreement that there are certain functions for which the right and left hemispheres of the brain take responsibility. Most significant for us is the agreement that the right brain deals with "wholeness" or the big picture, whereas the left brain operates at a linear, analytical level of detail.

… the axons in the right brain are longer than in the left and this means that they connect neurons that are, on average, further away from one another. Given that neurons that do similar things or process particular types of input tend to be clustered together, this suggests that the right brain is better equipped than the left to draw on several different brain modules at the same time. The long-range neural wiring might explain why that hemisphere is inclined to come out with broad, many-faceted, but rather vague concepts. It might also help the right brain to integrate sensory and emotional stimuli and to make the sort of unlikely connections that provide the basis for much humor. "Lateral thinking" would be helped, too, by the neural arrangement in the right brain – the sideways extension of axons even makes the phrase literal rather than figurative.

Rita Carter

From the perspective of a teacher, the most important point is to acknowledge is that there is a big picture – a whole – and that there are parts that make up the whole. This may seem obvious, but in fact many schools currently do not teach students "the big picture"; instead emphasis is on the linear presentation of discrete units of information. Our understanding reflects our ability to place new information inside a bigger picture; mapping supports the teacher and learner in doing this because the whole *and* the parts that make up the whole are present at the same time.

As individuals, we have different learning style preferences. Perhaps it is a person's style of thinking and learning that causes differences in the electrical activity of the two sides of his brain. There is a plethora of learning style inventories available to use. Educational psychologists Riding and Rayner carried out a major study in this area, looking at data from as far back as the 1940s. They examined the different words people used to describe functions and analyzed the constructs they employed, and then synthesized this knowledge. The result was a two-dimensional map of cognitive styles that encompassed the distinctions used in the other inventories. The two dimensions are "wholist–analytic" and "verbalizer–imager".

Below is a similar map to illustrate the dimensions of thinking inherent in the process of creating a map. The organization of material into the hierarchically structured branches of a map demands an analytic perspective, while the attention paid to the overall balance and significance of the big picture is represented by the wholist end of this dimension. The use of keywords requires a verbalizer style of thinking, while the inclusion of icons draws on the mapper's skills as an imager. Model maps would seem, therefore, to reflect a balanced cognitive style.

Brain imaging studies confirm that the two hemispheres really do have quite specific skills that are "hard-wired" to the extent that, in normal circumstances, certain skills will always develop on a particular side ... The right hemisphere is also good at grasping wholes, while the left brain likes details ... The tasks that each hemisphere takes on are those that fit its style of working: holistic or analytical ... They each process their "halves" of the big picture, and then pool their information.

Rita Carter

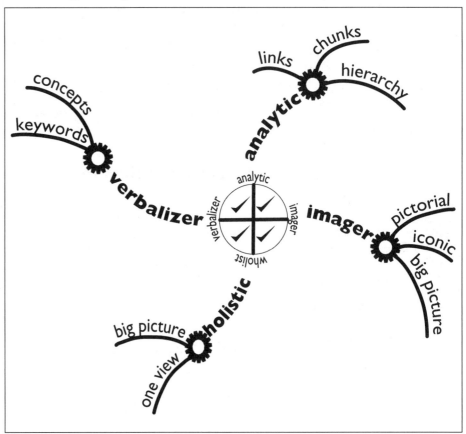

Concept mapping works extremely well for children who are visual learners and for those who are spatially, linguistically, or logically intelligent.

Mrs. Shahida Chowdhury, Teacher

... for imagers, mental pictures are likely to be less stable than those produced by verbalizers since they will be liable to interference and displacement by further involuntary intrusive images.

Riding and *Rayner*

This is not how maps are usually viewed. People often dismiss maps of any sort on the assertion that they are not "visual learners". Put simply, because the first sense to engage a map is sight, there is an assumption that they best support visual "imager" learners and not auditory or kinesthetic learners.

Riding and Rayner point to research that shows that non-imagers are in fact more successful in establishing stable mental images and are better at producing drawings from memory than their more "visual" peers. There is an argument, therefore, that maps may actually be more effective for verbalizers than for imagers – the very opposite to the popular view.

In the authors' experience, it is not helpful to allocate specific activities exclusively to people appearing to fall within one of the identified categories of learners. For the student, this can lead to the construction of a belief that is not empowering. "Beliefs arise from your unwillingness to trust direct experience," asserts Smothermon – in fact, Wenger claims, 80% of the brain's function is "visual", even for those with presumed auditory or kinesthetic preferences, so we should not allow ourselves or our students to be restricted by specific labels. As Bannister suggests, "personal learning myths [about one's preferred learning style] become a handicap to effective learning". Sternberg, a foremost analyst of thinking styles, reminds us that "Styles are teachable. For the most part, people acquire their styles through socialization. But it is also possible to teach styles". He suggests teachers can do this by modelling the styles themselves and explaining the advantages of each different way of thinking and learning.

Differentiated instruction implies activities that appeal to students' learning preference — visual, kinesthetic or auditory. When you provide visual, auditory and kinesthetic activities you are increasing the likelihood that your students will make a connection between a current stimulus and previous experience and understanding.

Visual learning

A presentation of your thinking as a map is the most visual form of input your students could receive.

Students are often subjected to what has been termed "one-pass learning" – as the teacher delivers information orally, they have to grasp and retain it immediately; the teacher's spoken word, if not captured, is quickly lost. The sequencing of information in this kind of spoken communication is necessarily linear, which means students have to maintain constant attention to follow the "story"; if that attention is broken, the students have no obvious means of picking up the thread again.

These problems are resolved with the use of maps. Maps are static and allow the student the chance to assimilate and reflect on the information. Visual information, unlike the spoken word, is not structured by time. That is to say, what you said five minutes ago can be viewed, with a map, at the same time as what you are saying right now. Students can review what has been said and place new information into a structure to give it meaning. The primary task of a student in receiving your delivery is to make sense of it – and she does this by referring it to past knowledge. When that knowledge is visible in front of her, the task is far more easily accomplished.

Auditory learning

For most, teaching primarily involves speaking and listening. Explanation is at the heart of teaching. While it is subject to time, in the sense that one spoken idea has to follow another, speaking can also transcend time because the speaker can move readily from current information to past knowledge. To follow such jumps can be intellectually interesting and exciting, but it runs the risk of losing the listener. With the backup of a visual "big picture" map, you need not limit the adventurous nature of your spoken delivery. Maps can support such flights because everyone is able to see, literally, where it is you have gone in your speaking. Your jumps are made visible and therefore traceable, so that learners can literally "see" what you are saying.

Kinesthetic learning

Thinking aloud involves talking through your thinking. When it is used in explaining a map, it becomes a very powerful way of integrating kinesthetic input into your teaching. For example, as you talk through your map with a class and explain the thinking behind its organization, you can also physically "walk" your finger along the branches. Your students can follow your thinking with their own fingers on their own maps as you demonstrate your explanation. The activity as a whole therefore appeals to students with any learning preference, visual, auditory or kinesthetic; they can see the map, hear your explanation and move their hands.

This seems a perfect encouragement to teachers to learn the skills of mapping and to demonstrate its fun and effectiveness to their students. Just as Tony Buzan did, students must at some stage expect their teachers to tell them how their brain works and to suggest ways of working that are exciting and "brain-friendly". Mapping has enormous benefits that students will want to hear about.

Benefits of mapping

Students want to know how they can

- create their own interest in a subject
- sustain concentration and comprehend content
- organize information
- stimulate memory.

The consistent use of mapping can significantly enhance these skills. When a map is constructed, the mapper is intensely involved in organizing information. As she does this, she gets to the core of the subject, investigating how it "clicks", and what concepts hold it together. It becomes a puzzle. Even the most uninspiring of topics can be transformed into areas of curiosity when mapping. The dullest of lengthy and bureaucratic meetings can be turned from a potentially gruelling experience into something of value – even of interest – using mapping.

When a new topic is presented too quickly, and the information cannot be linked to your existing body of knowledge, you soon lose interest because the new material has no meaning to you. Mapping allows you to place it into your existing framework, starting the process of "meaning-making". Once this process starts, interest soon follows. You could say that mapping follows the dictum "fake it till you make it". Your map is your invention and as such will always offer you the possibility of fun, however little the subject or lecturer appears to be offering you.

We all find it very hard to sustain our focus – especially when faced with a blank sheet of paper and trying to formulate "the beginning". The trouble is that linear, sequential text has shaped our beliefs that we must always conform to that format. Learning is dependent on images and holographic thinking, but education is currently dependent on language skills and linear thinking. So teachers and students spend a great deal of effort tearing themselves away from an area of interest and forcing themselves to focus on the "next thing" on a linear agenda, rather than making the most of the natural inclination to seek stimulation by scanning, getting an overview and experimenting in seeing new connections.

Mapping supports this natural cycle of concentration. In fact, it doesn't even feel like concentration; it feels like involvement and interest. Mapping allows, even encourages, you to follow the flow of your thoughts. It supports what could be negatively interpreted as "flitting around". But the interpretation depends on the intention. The mapper has the intention of understanding the topic, or of creating something new, and in this context "flitting around" becomes an asset. Within the context of having to follow a very determined path of focus (linear text), "flitting around" becomes negatively viewed; and that may reveal the reason why so many of our students are having problems in schools.

If there is one thing we can predict with certainty, it is that we will be dealing with larger amounts of ever more complex information in the future. Mapping gets to the heart of information management. Its very structure is dependent on analyzing information and categorizing content into related and hierarchically ordered branches. This process is the very essence of understanding.

With experience, you will be able to "tame" the most daunting of collections of information, using mapping. As you become more proficient, you will be more aware of the exact questions you need to ask to understand the topic more fully. Your map provides very real and direct feedback on how well you are organizing information – if there is an item that you cannot categorize, it becomes very clear what you must find out to complete your understanding.

This awareness of being the author of the "story" of your map, resulting from your powers of organizing information, alters your relationship to learning. The relationship of the mapper to the teacher is also radically changed.

Memory can be easily shaped and improved using memory strategies. For the most part, these relate to short- and medium-term retention of content, and can be categorized under the term "rote learning". While rote learning does have a part to play in education, by far the greater part is played by "meaningful learning", as Novak has argued so eloquently over the past 20 years.

Medium-term memory is very much supported by the use of categorization. Back in 1969, an experiment entitled "Hierarchical retrieval schemes in recall of categorized word lists" showed just that. It showed just how effective it is to put words into groups with a common attribute. The words, however, were not necessarily meaningful. That is to say, they were not related to a subject under study. They did not form a narrative, and so give meaning. Isolated words have to be worked on, for example by connecting them to numbers, outrageous images or humorous narrative. In this way, they can be committed to

… so-called memory tricks and other "superlearning" strategies have little or nothing to do with meaningful learning; such promulgations are usually characterized by their avoidance of any discussion of the conceptual nature of knowledge and the strategies by which humans construct knowledge.

J. D. Novak and *D. B. Gowin*

Information learned by rote (nonsense syllables and meaningless word pairs) cannot be anchored to major elements in cognitive structure and hence form a minimum linkage within it. Unless materials learned by rote are restudied repeatedly to achieve overlearning … they cannot be recalled several hours or several days after learning. Information that is learned meaningfully (associated with subsumers and cognitive structure) can usually be recalled for weeks or months after acquisition.

Joseph Novak

medium-term memory. Education should not be a content-driven, teach–test cycle, in which success can be achieved using medium-term memory tricks alone. For something to stay in a student's long-term memory, and therefore be useful in life and not just in the next exam, it must be meaningful to that student.

Mapping to develop reading and writing skills

For many years, experts in reading comprehension have advocated methodology consistent with mapping. Reading comprehension depends upon activating prior knowledge about text, fitting what is in the text to what students already know about the subject of a text. Effective readers set their purpose and make predictions before they read. As they read, they employ strategies including predicting, visualizing, summarizing and questioning. After reading, effective readers paraphrase, check predictions, answer questions and re-check text to refine their interpretations. Effective readers are metacognitive in that they are able to identify and select strategies which aid their comprehension. Mapping can be a valuable tool in building background knowledge and setting purpose for reading. Maps built during and after reading help readers monitor the sense they are making of text and to note important aspects of text.

Semantic mapping has long been recognized as a sound, visual strategy for expanding one's vocabulary because new words are related to concepts and to familiar words. Creating a semantic map with students combines the advantage of total student involvement with brain-compatible learning. The magic of semantic mapping emerges when students see "old" words in a new light, when they see how "new" words relate to "old" words. Since vocabulary instruction is most effective when it is wedded to the learner's prior knowledge, teachers have good reason to emphasize mapping when students are expected to learn new vocabulary. For this very reason, experts in English-as-a-second-language instruction have recently emphasized mapping as an important instructional technique.

Mapping can also be employed as a pre-writing strategy and to facilitate for oral presentations. Effective writing depends upon planning and building or activating background knowledge during pre-writing, keeping the flow throughout drafting and revising for clarity, organization, vocabulary and sentence patterns as well as matters of spelling, punctuation and grammar knowledge. Students who build maps before they write set themselves up for success in drafting and revision. They quickly recognize the need for further information related to their purpose and audience. Insights developed throughout the writing process result in revisions to original maps, a testament to the link between writing and learning. Similarly, maps help students prepare and present orally. Maps formatted on cards, charts or overhead transparencies facilitate the comprehension of listeners in the audience.

Not all students are able to identify the main organizing principles for an essay or project. Therefore, it can be useful to discuss the assignment with the group as a pre-writing activity:

1. What is your purpose? Your topic? Your writing or presentational format? Place this at the centre of the map.
2. Who is your audience?

3. What are the main branches of your map? You could provide a template for students with these branches already present with the challenge for students to create sub-branches. Ideally, students should independently determine the branches and sub-branches for their writing presentational task.

The following map was created by a grade 8 student who struggled with his writing. Look at the way he organized his knowledge about sport. Examine the vocabulary he has used. Look at the spellings he has attempted. The map illustrates the difference that mapping can make to an individual who has had difficulty in organizing his thoughts – both in terms of his ability to make sense of the information but also the differences it made to his feelings about himself as a learner.

Another example on page 22 is provided by a junior high E.S.L. student. Note how the student has used a map to plan and compose a character sketch. The character's name is in the centre of the map. The main branches focus on character traits. The sub-branches focus on details from the story to illustrate the character's traits.

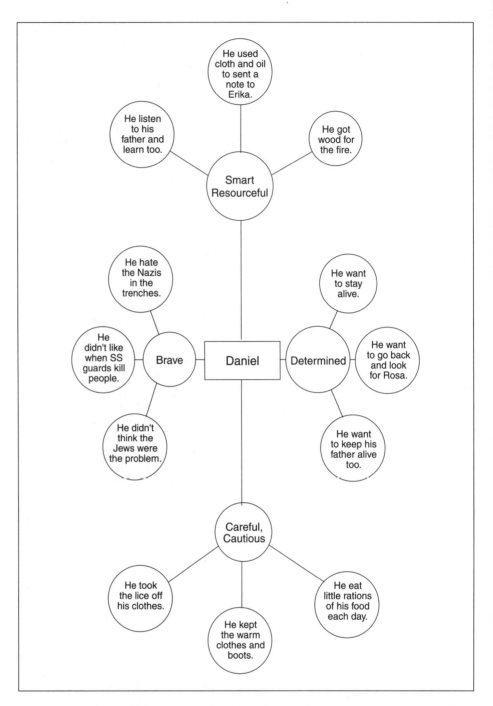

Maps are a perfect summary of the meaning made of a subject. Additionally, as described earlier in this chapter, maps offer vital visual hooks for recall. All the aspects of recall so beloved of memory experts can be found in maps – the strong images, the color, the humor, the associations, the variety of size, contrast and texture – but they are placed within an organized network of meaning.

Note-making and note-taking

For writers, the contrast between linear text and maps is significant. Being based on the organizing structure of the topic itself, maps are created "out of time"; that is, they are not confined by the sequential and linear nature of time-related delivery of text or aural stimulus.

Taking notes at a lecture highlights this contrast beautifully. However disorganized and confusing the speaker, whatever her manner of jumping around from point to unrelated point, the mapper proceeds by methodically charting out the major concepts while at the same time grouping and organizing the details. A discontinuous leap by a speaker is easily assimilated into the growing "big picture". Furthermore, subsequent additions can be made to the map that amplify details or themes or links.

Mapping a speaker who is very organized in her delivery – who has organized her talk into sections and her sections into sub-sections – is, however, much easier than mapping someone who jumps about. The point is that a mapper can cope with the jumping about because he is not restricted to writing in a linear, "down the page" way. He can jump about with the speaker!

Working in this way is completely different to normal note-taking, which more closely resembles dictation followed by handwriting practice. Mappers are very active listeners of, and indeed participants in, the lecture. They constantly search to make sense of what they are hearing, turning data into information. By forming hierarchies of categories, they hypothesize whether such conceptual groupings best summarize the topic. And that summary will be shaped by the purpose of the note-taker. A lecture can be interpreted in several ways and so the mapper will be aware of the need to create a structure that best suits his own "information need".

A mapper may spend some time considering what it is he wants to achieve in order to establish his main organizing principles. If his task is to produce an accurate summary of the speech, video or programme, he will try to establish what the main points of the stimulus are. If the mapper is attending a lecture or course, he may ask the course presenter what the main topics to be covered will be.

Maps, unlike linear text, are easily reformatted or redrawn if new information or a fresh insight opens up the possibility of a new structure. After a lecture, a map is a very powerful tool to test out your personal grasp of the topic with your fellow learners, or indeed the lecture. A map is a perfect basis upon which to ask questions that test both what the mapper thinks she has understood, and what she has not been able to "place" (i.e. contextualize) onto the map. Maps are "public", "concrete" and "memorable" in a way that linear notes are not.

Note-making, as opposed to note-taking, is the construction of a plan for writing, public speaking, project creation or any other pursuit that is your "invention". Here, we see a comically similar image of the systematic and vigorous note-taker following the meanderings of an undisciplined lecturer; this time, though, the lecturer is replaced by your own mind.

In traditional note-making, we try to "discipline" our mind by forcing it to produce thoughts in sequential fashion, even rejecting good ideas because they haven't appeared in the correct order. The mapper does no such thing. He accepts all good ideas whenever they appear because they are quickly and efficiently put into convenient and appropriate space on the map. In this way the mapper works *with* the mind and not *against* it. While being able to deal with spontaneously tempting thoughts, the mapper will find that the visual structure of the model will concentrate his attention on the aspect being examined. It is as if the pattern of the map draws in the attention of the viewer and combines the powers of sight and thought. A real sense of momentum is felt as the categories, links and relationships develop.

In this "brain-friendly" and productive environment, creativity flourishes. From apparently nowhere, ideas and novel connections appear. It is no wonder that mappers find both note-taking and note-making engaging, stimulating, interesting and fun. Mappers, in fact, have an increased capacity for learning.

Use it or lose it

Armed with these skills and working from such a firm basis of confidence and enjoyment, mappers are keen to exploit the technique in as many ways as possible. They report with enthusiasm how they have used mapping to

- take notes from books, lectures, videos or computer programmes
- take notes in an interview situation or telephone conversation
- take minutes at a meeting
- organize writing and oral presentations
- comprehend reading, content and learn vocabulary
- make a display
- plan a budget, a project or a shopping trip
- plan a day / week / month / term / year
- create a new idea
- solve a problem
- tell and analyze a story.

This list could be almost endless. After all, if you were to list all the applications of writing linear text, where would you stop? It is almost the same with mapping. People find mapping to be

- a faster and truer way of translating a thought onto paper than copying
- a way of supporting scanning text from a book
- a facilitative way of creating
- a way of realizing how you are forming your thoughts, which some call "helicoptering" and others call "metacognition"
- open-ended in the way it allows for further contributions to be added
- more orderly than linear text, despite the apparent random configuration of branches
- perfectly suited for simultaneous co-operative work
- a way of working with many items without have to remember items listed on previous pages
- an easier way to handle complex ideas and issues.

You are now fully informed and ready to map. When you have learned to map (see chapter 2), and you begin to experience the benefits, you too will want to look for more areas in which to apply the technique. Remember, "Maps aren't mirrors of reality; they are a means of understanding it".

2 How to map

mapping demystified, deconstructed and put back together again

How many times have you read step-by-step instructions that left you just as baffled at the end as you were before you started? The promise of learning a new skill in "10 easy lessons" lures you into the process and you keep going because you are assured that all will become clear at the end.

There are currently courses and books available to teach you how to map, but each has its own shortfalls. The procedure described in this chapter fills the gaps left by other texts, and has been used successfully by International MBA Students, teachers and students of all ages and abilities (including students with moderate learning difficulties). It will work for you too.

To help you find your way, the chapter is divided into the following sections:

- Keywords and language hierarchies
- Organizing principles
- Holographics
- Step-by-step guides for mapping

Keywords and language hierarchies

When we listen to someone speaking, or read a book, there are some words that we must pick up and understand if we are to make sense of the whole. These are keywords. The sentence "Please get me a coffee" is completely meaningless without the keywords "coffee" and, to a lesser degree, "get" – the other words are not vital. It is keywords that are used in the construction of maps.

In classrooms, keywords may well be specific to the subject being taught. They are primarily nouns, often verbs and sometimes adjectives, associated with the attitudes, skills and information under study. Unless children can identify relationships between keywords, understanding will be limited. But, of course, before they can identify relationships, they have to be able to identify the keywords themselves – this is a skill that both reflects the student's level of understanding and develops it.

The importance of being able to identify keywords can be illustrated by imagining two people as filing cabinets.

In the first filing cabinet information to be stored is selected randomly with no regard to purpose or contexts, past, present or future. In this filing cabinet no attention is paid to where this randomly selected information is placed. No understanding of the information is given and no meaning has been created. It is simply jammed in along with every other piece of information that has preceded it.

In the second cabinet information is selected carefully with due consideration to the purpose and contexts from which it has come and into which it is to be placed. Keywords are identified and create meaning for the user. Careful attention is given to ensuring that the information is then stored in files that reflect the understanding and meaning created by the person. Clearly the selection and organization of information has a direct influence on the "user friendliness" of the filing cabinet.

Ours minds are like filing cabinets, packed with information. The only difference between us is that some of us are better at filing than others.

Exercises: identifying and using keywords

The following exercises have been designed for readers, especially teachers, to learn about keywords and related mapping strategies. Chapter 3 focuses on instructional approaches related to these exercises.

To have any expectations at all demands some kind of filing system – demands, in other words, the setting up of categories of experience.

James Britton

Name: _____

Worksheet 1: using keywords in writing

Think back to a vacation or a day out that you really enjoyed. Remember as much detail as possible about your visit and write as much as you can on the lines below. (You can also use the back of this sheet.) Write about the location, the weather, people, travel arrangements, food, feelings, thoughts, funniest / scariest / best / worst moments or anything else that you can recall. Keep going until it would be impossible to fit all of your writing onto a postcard, even if you were able to type the information, reduce it in size and then stick it on! Now put this piece of paper aside and read on – we will return to your trip after the next exercise.

_____
_____
_____
_____
_____
_____
_____
_____
_____
_____
_____
_____
_____
_____
_____
_____
_____
_____
_____
_____
_____
_____

Name: _____

Worksheet 2: the importance of nouns

Below is an extract from a book, in which the nouns, verbs and adjectives have been left out. Read the extract and then try to guess what the extract is about.

_____, the _____ _____ of a _____ _____ a lot of _____ from the _____ on the _____ and _____. Perhaps our _____ _____ towards _____ _____ in our _____ through _____ _____ and _____ _____ is _____. In _____ for the _____ and _____ of _____ _____ we _____ _____ for the _____ of the _____ and _____ _____ that _____ _____ of our _____ _____. We are all _____.

It's difficult to make any sense of the extract with so much missing. Now try this version, with only the nouns and verbs missing.

_____, the school _____ of a _____ _____ a lot of _____ from the _____ on the _____ and _____. Perhaps our natural _____ towards _____ _____ in our _____ through visual _____ and spatial _____ is undervalued. In _____ for the _____ and _____ of _____ _____ we are _____ for the _____ of the visual and spatial _____ that _____ _____ of our neural _____. We are all _____.

Still, it is very hard to create any accurate meaning from the extract. Try it with only nouns missing.

_____, the school _____ of a _____ places a lot of _____ from the _____ on the _____ and _____. Perhaps our natural _____ towards organizing _____ in our _____ through visual _____ and spatial _____ is undervalued. In arguing for the _____ and _____ of _____ _____ we are arguing for the _____ of the visual and spatial _____ that seems _____ of our neural _____. We are all _____.

Even now, the meaning is far from clear. The point is that nouns carry more meanings and associations than any other words. Verbs also help us to understand and make meaning, as do adjectives, though to a lesser extent. But the words that help make most sense of the extract are nouns. Here is the full text to illustrate the point.

Nowadays, the school experience of a child places a lot of emphasis from the outset on the written and spoken. Perhaps our natural disposition towards organizing information in our heads through visual patterns and spatial relationships is undervalued. In arguing for the teaching and use of mapping techniques we are arguing for the extension of the visual and spatial propensity that seems part of our neural architecture. We are all mappers.

Name: _____

Worksheet 3: postcard map

Now let's go back to Worksheet 1. Highlight all the nouns, verbs and adjectives in your writing about your trip. If you were to write these words alone on a postcard, how much information about your trip would the recipient be able to glean from it if the words were arranged as in the examples shown?

Using these postcards as a model, try arranging the highlighted words from your writing in the blank postcard below.

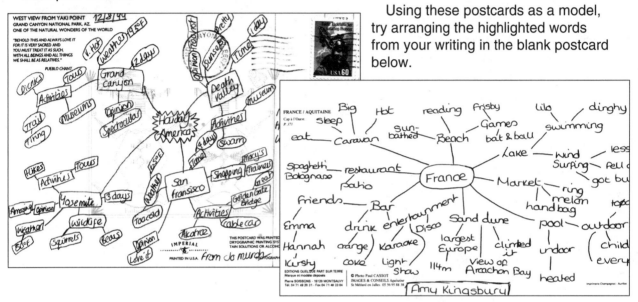

Place Stamp Here

Keywords in language hierarchies

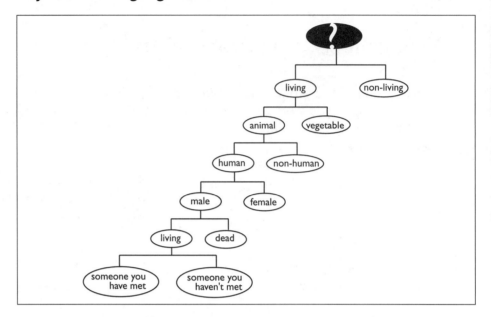

Having an understanding of the hierarchical relationships between word meanings will help you select and use keywords in your maps. It will also mean that you (and your students) will be able to discern relationships between concepts represented through language (keywords) on your maps. In so doing you will be learning meaningfully.

Visually, we can represent this hierarchical ordering of language as a triangle. The diagram shown is an example of this.

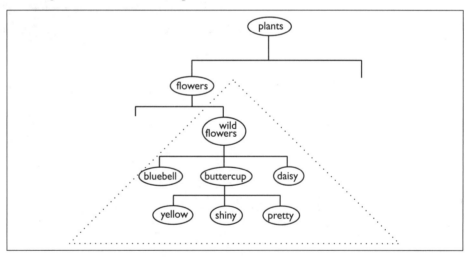

Towards the bottom of the triangle hierarchy we have some common names of some specific flowers – "buttercup", "bluebell" and "daisy". If we think of "buttercup", we may think of the words "yellow", "shiny" and "pretty". These words come to mind *after* thinking of "buttercup". When we think of "wild flowers", we do not think of "yellow", "shiny" and "pretty" until after we have thought of the names of wild flowers, specifically "buttercup". Above "wild flowers" on the hierarchy, we have "flowers", and above this "plants"; if we think of the word "plants" we are even less likely to think "yellow", "shiny" and "pretty".

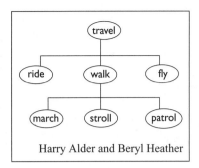

Harry Alder and Beryl Heather

So, we only think of the descriptive words related to the buttercup after we have thought of the buttercup. Notice the higher up the language triangle we travel, the more abstract or general the terminology becomes.

All words can be organized into hierarchies. The diagram on the left illustrates this beautifully.

The conceptual level of the language we use has to be sufficiently high to be able to group together all the "things", "ideas" and "actions" of the concept being examined. However, if we go too high up the hierarchy we may lose many of the associations that occur at the level we're interested in. For example, if we were to ask a student to write a story about her pet, Rover, it would be useful for the student to tells us that Rover is a dog and that he is one of several furry domestic pets at home. For the purpose of the story, however, it is not necessary for the student to tell us that Rover is a mammal. There is a danger of "over-conceptualizing". The level at which we enter the language hierarchy in essence depends on the purpose for which we are using the language.

This does not mean you should pick words from the upper levels of the staircase [hierarchy], where you find the abstract or general words. It might equally be concrete details that give you the best associations.

I. Svantesson

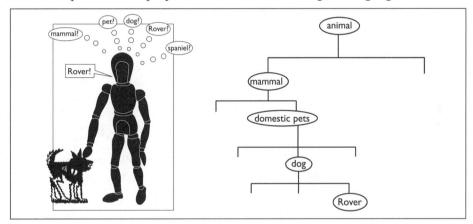

Generally speaking, at the bottom of language hierarchies we tend to have specific details of language. As we move towards the top of the hierarchy we move towards less specific and more general words that can overlap or encompass the words below. In effect, we move from a concrete level of detailed language at the bottom to an abstract level at the top.

Another example of hierarchical levels of language is shown in the diagram below.

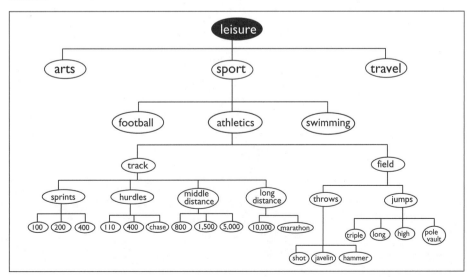

Terms like "javelin", "100 metres" and "pole vault" may release in our minds words associated with these events. The words "track" and "field" could release not only the events given above (javelin etc.) but also other associated events – these words are at a higher level on our language triangle, and so have more terms subordinate to them.

As we proceed further up the triangle, we reach a greater level of abstraction. You cannot *see* "athletics" – you can only see examples of athletics events. Similarly, you cannot *see* "track events" or "field events" – you can only see examples of them. If you were asked to plan a talk about "athletics" you would not include football or cricket (although, of course, players of these sports are athletes of their own discipline). If, however, you were asked to plan a talk about "sport" you could include athletics, football and cricket within your selection. The level at which you enter the hierarchy depends upon your purpose.

When you create a map, you are setting down the language hierarchy associated with the concept under examination. The part of the hierarchy you use in your map depends upon your purpose. The associations you make within your map may well be different from those in the example above, but the key is to ensure that they are arranged hierarchically – each new word should be "contained" within the concept word to which you attach it (as "track" is contained within "athletics", and "pole vault" is contained within "jumps"). (See Medal Collecting map on page 107.)

When mapping, it is important to imagine language triangles as you are working with your subject area. Ask yourself:

- What words would I associate under this?
- Is this the best word to use, or is there another word that contains this one in it?
- Is there a group of words that this word is part of?

With practice, you will become adept at choosing the word that best releases all the associated ideas beneath.

Exercises: placing words into language hierarchies

It is tempting when you start mapping to think that you need to use lots of keywords in order to record information – you don't. These exercises are designed to help select keywords by "seeing" and using language triangles.

Name: _____

Worksheet 4: creating language triangles

Complete the following language triangles by writing a keyword on each line that would link all the words underneath the line together. The first one is done for you. Then create your own language triangles for parts 7 and 8.

1.
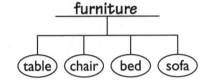

2.

3.
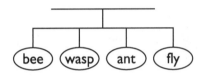

4.
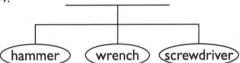

5.
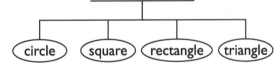

6.
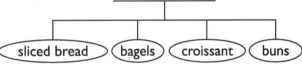

7.

8.

Name: _____

Worksheet 5: using language triangles to map

You will need three or four sheets of paper to do this exercise.

1. Draw a small circle in the middle of a page, with lines radiating out from it. Write the word "exercise" in the circle. Follow the model given in example A. to "brainstorm" words you associate with "exercise", and write them on the radiating lines. It does not matter if your words are not the same as those in the example.

2. Next, on another sheet of paper, group together words that you associate with one another. In example B., the words "individual", "team" and "weights" are grouped together.

3. Now try to identify the keyword that would link all the words in each group together. See example C. If you cannot identify a word that links or associates them all together check to see if they do, in fact, go together. Sometimes you will need to move words to another group or start another category altogether. In example C., the word "types" is used to group together the words "team", "individual" and "weights" – they are all different types of exercise. Can you think of any other types of exercise that you could add?

4. Now think back to the language hierarchies we were looking at earlier. What information could you add at the bottom of this "triangle"? In other words, what examples of "team", "individual" or "weights" exercise could you add?

As you can see, the keywords used to organize the information in example C. are written near the centre of the map, and are not necessarily contained within the original brainstorm. We have to go "higher" up the language hierarchy to find words to organize the information most effectively.

A.

B.

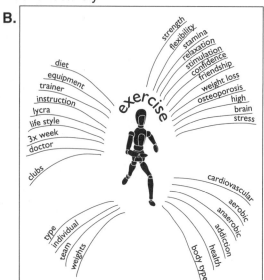

C.

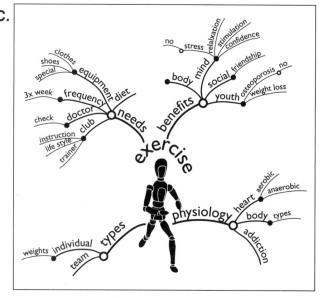

Organizing principles

You may be thinking that there must be hundreds of different ways that we can organize information. Relax – there are, in fact, only five ways, and each of them will permit a different understanding of the information. The following are applicable to any endeavor.

- **Category** – goods are organized by category or model in a shop
- **Time** – used for organizing items associated with events over a fixed duration; for example, museums, exhibitions and historical accounts are organized in this way
- **Location** – used to examine and compare information originating from different sources
- **Alphabet** – often used to organize large bodies of information; since we all know the alphabet, it is accessible to all, while other classifications may not be
- **Continuum** – organization by magnitude, such as "small to large", "least expensive to most expensive", "least important to most important" and so on.

Exercises: organizing information

The following exercises on pages 36–38 (Worksheets 6–8) are designed to help you organize information when mapping.

Uncovering the organizing principles is like having the ultimate hatrack. It is essential when working with already existing bodies of information, as it is in developing your own information. The time spent comprehending someone else's method of organization will reduce the search time spent looking for individual components.

Richard Saul Wurman

Name: _____

Worksheet 6: organization of lizards

Below are four lizards, labelled a, b, c, d, that need organizing. Do parts 1 and 2 of the exercise to indicate how the lizards could be organized according to size and color. Then complete part 3 to show how they could be organized by size and color.

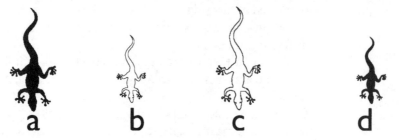

1. **Write a, b, c, or d in the empty squares to organize the lizards by size.**

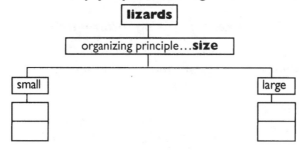

2. **Write a, b, c, or d in the empty squares to organize the lizards by color.**

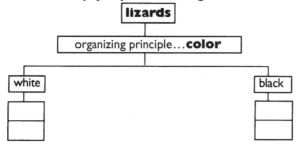

3. **Write a, b, c or d in the empty squares to organize the lizards by size and color.**

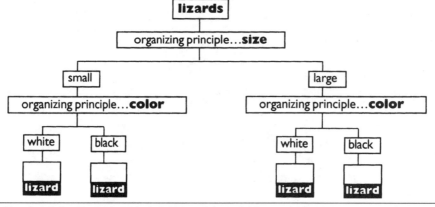

Name: ____________________________

Worksheet 7: organization of monsters

Below are four monsters labelled a, b, c, d that need organizing. Follow the instructions given below to complete parts 1, 2, 3 and 4.

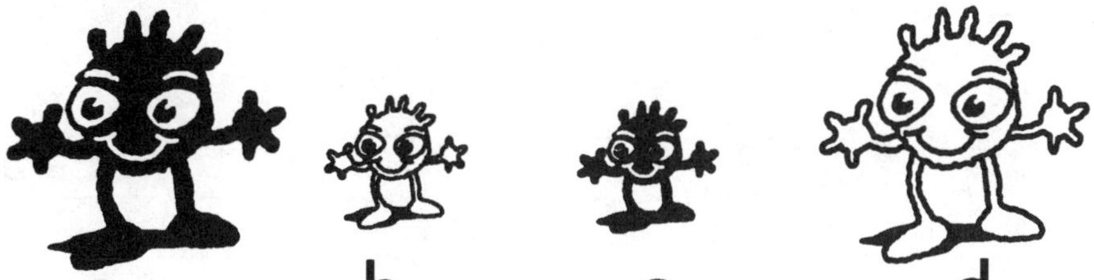

a b c d

1. Fill in what is missing...

- White monsters... ___ and ___
- Black monsters... ___ and ___
- Large monsters... ___ and ___
- Small monsters... ___ and ___

- Monster a is... *black and large*
- Monster b is... ____________
- Monster c is... ____________
- Monster d is... ____________

2.

- Which monster is small and white? _______
- Which monster is black and large? _______
- What do monsters b and d have in common? ____________________
- What do monsters a and d have in common? ____________________
- Which pairs of monsters are different both in color and size?
  pair ____ and ____ and pair ____ and ____

3. Complete the following table...

color			
black	white		
		small	size
		large	size

4. Organize the monsters by size and color by completing the chart below.

- Fill in the headings and write the correct letter in each empty square.
- The organizing principles are now not written down. They still work in the same way but only the characteristics (white, black, large, small) are written.

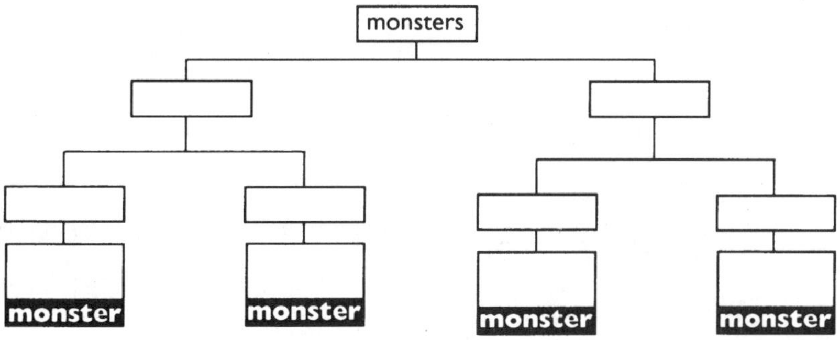

Name: _____

Worksheet 8: organization of geometric shapes

Below are shapes that need organizing. Complete parts 1 and 2 to establish how the shapes could be organized. Then complete part 3 to show how to classify the shapes according to shape, color and size.

1. Fill in the table...

Number	Shape	Size	Color
1			
2			
3			
4			
5			
6			
7			
8			
9			
10			
11			
12			

2. Establishing organizing principles

- How many different **shapes** have you found? _____
- What are they?

_____

- How many different **sizes** have you found? _____
- What are they?

_____

- How many different **colors** have you found? _____
- What are they?

_____

3. Organization according to shape, size and color

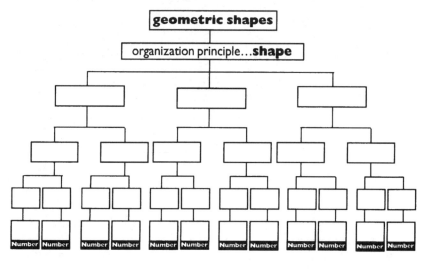

Holographics

The following exercises on pages 40–44 (Worksheets 9–13) are designed to take you from linear to holographic thinking, and thereby help you use your classification skills in the production of maps.

Exercises: classifying information

Look at the mapping classification of a shoe shop below. At the top is shown one possible classification tree for a shoe shop. The main classification of the stock is by intended wearer – the shoes are divided up under "male", "female" and "children". Beneath the classification "male" the shoes are classified into "types"; namely "sports", "casual" and "dress". (The same classification could have been used for "female" and "children", but for the purpose of the exercise only the "male" shoes have been classified.) The classification tree goes on to show the organization of the shoes according to color and size.

Below the tree is a map of the same information. The subject of the classification, "shoes", is at the centre and the main organizing or classification principles – namely "male", "female" and "children" – radiate from the centre. The organizing principles of male shoes – "sports", "casual" and "dress" – then branch off from "male". Note that there is room to classify the "female" and "children" shoes in the same way here if required, whereas there was little space in the classification tree. The same information is represented in a different way.

Ultimately this is what a map is: a series of key ideas or principles stemming from, and classified around, a central theme or data.

On pages 40–44, (Worksheets 9–13), other information has been classified and then represented in a map, in the same way as for the shoe shop. However, in each map key information has been omitted. Complete each map by filling in the missing information.

The purpose of these exercises is twofold. First, it is to help you see that maps are effectively a series of classifications around a central point. Second, it provides you with the opportunity to start writing and representing information in a new way. As you work through the exercises ask yourself these questions:

- In what other ways could this information have been organized?
- Where else in my life do I already organize information like this?

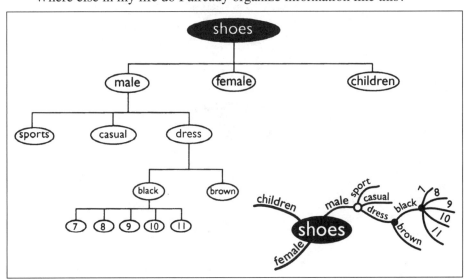

Worksheet 9: classification of a supermarket

Below is a classification tree of a supermarket. Below the classification tree is a map representing the same information, however, key information is missing from the map. Complete the map by filling in the missing information.

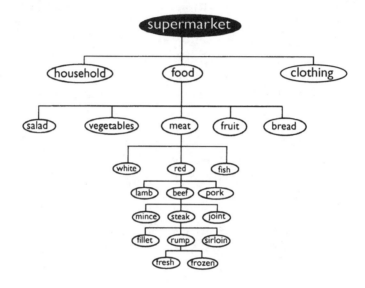

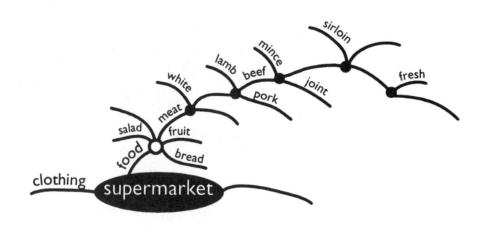

Name: _____

Worksheet 10: classification of pets

Below is a classification tree of pets. Below the classification tree is a map representing the same information, however, key information is missing from the map. Complete the map by filling in the missing information.

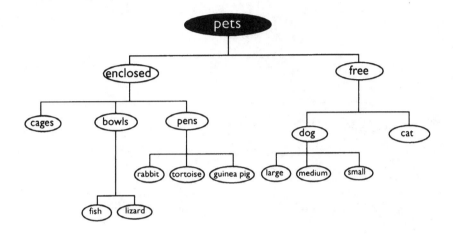

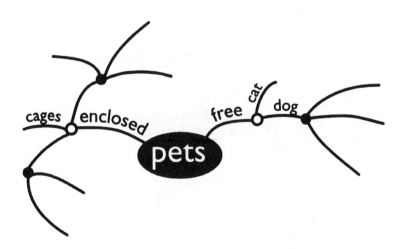

Name: _____

Worksheet 11: classification of sports day

Below is a classification tree of a sports day. Below the classification tree is a map representing the same information, however, key information is missing from the map. Complete the map by filling in the missing information.

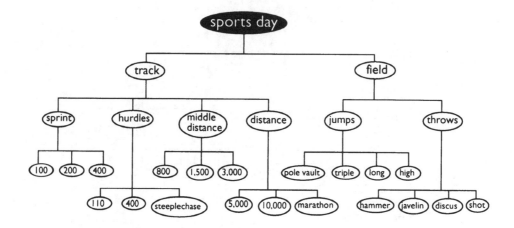

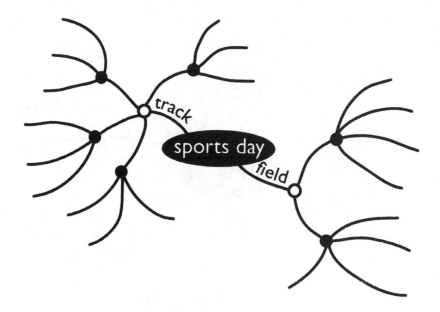

Name: _____

Worksheet 12: classification of life

Below is a classification tree illustrating the different kinds of life. Below the classification tree is a map representing the same information, however, key information is missing from the map. Complete the map by filling in the missing information.

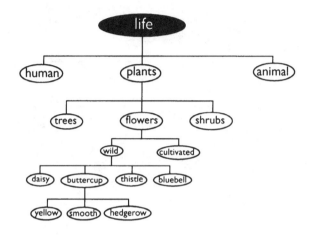

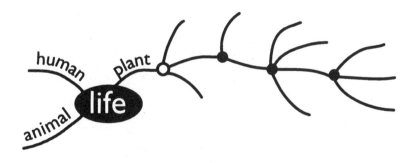

Name: _____

Worksheet 13: classification of transportation

Below is a classification tree showing different kinds of transportation. On your own, create a map using the information provided in the classification tree.

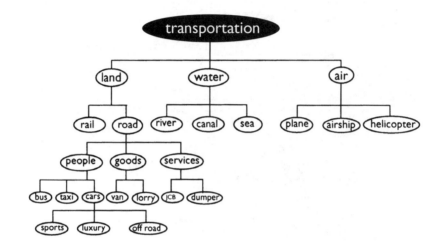

Step-by-step guides for mapping

The map on page 49 is about the benefits of mapping. This section takes you through the thinking that took place to produce this map – it *models* the authors' thinking. Where keywords used on the map appear here in the text, they are in bold type, to model the selection and use of keywords within a map.

1. We started by asking ourselves these questions:

    - What is the purpose of the map?
    - In what context is to be used?

   The context for the map was an educational leaflet to be distributed to schools. Its purpose was to illustrate the benefits of mapping in a way that was readily understandable (without additional explanation) to its audience – the teaching profession.

2. Being clear about the purpose from the start helped us to decide later which information to put in and which to leave out. It also meant we were able to come up with a title for our map that would itself be the main organizing principle. The title – Benefits – came to us during the discussion since all the ideas we wanted to communicate came under this heading. We placed the word "**benefits**" at the centre of the page.

3. We then had to decide what the main organizing principles would be for our map – we had to establish what the main branches from the centre would contain. We quickly decided that we wanted to focus on **teaching** and **learning** and so we added these branches to our map.

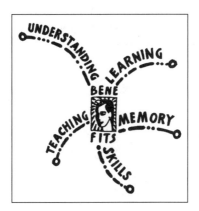

4. We then discussed what information we wanted to contain within these headings. We discussed how learning involves committing things to memory and in turn how long-term memory depends on actually **understanding** the concepts or information being learned. We also discussed how mapping supports the learner in creating interest, sustaining concentration, organizing information and shaping **memory**. The acquisition of these **skills** promotes certain qualities or attitudes in learners; it can make learners more resilient, resourceful and responsible for their work.

   Each of these three keywords – "understanding", "memory" and "skills" – needed further elaboration so at this point we faced a choice. We could either use them as sub-headings branching off from "learning", or we could emphasize their importance by giving them their own branches. As you can see, we decided on the latter. We now had five main branches.

5. We then moved randomly around the branches adding sub-headings as we discussed them. Because this account is written in linear form it is hard to recreate the random nature of our discussion but if we take each of the branches in turn we can walk you through our thinking.

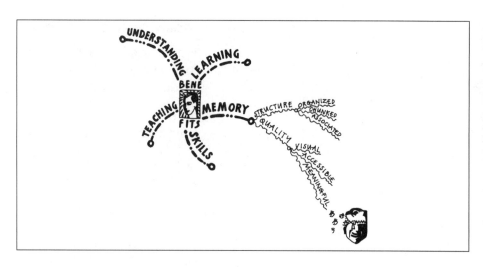

The "memory" branch

6. We decided that the two main reasons why mapping supports long-term memory are its **qualities** and its **structure**. We discussed having the structure of the map as one of the qualities – that is, having "structure" branching off from "qualities" – but because we wanted to emphasize the importance of structure, we gave it a separate branch off from "memory".

7. A map's structure is **organized** hierarchically so that the learner can see which information is contained within each section. It is **chunked** so that the learner can see which elements go together. This also helps the learner to see relationships within the whole. The fact that the whole is always visible supports the learner in making **associations** with other areas of the map.

8. We decided to emphasize three qualities of maps. First, research shows that our capacity for **visual** recall is vast. As each map, unlike linear text, is visually unique, so it helps us to remember. A map's layout means

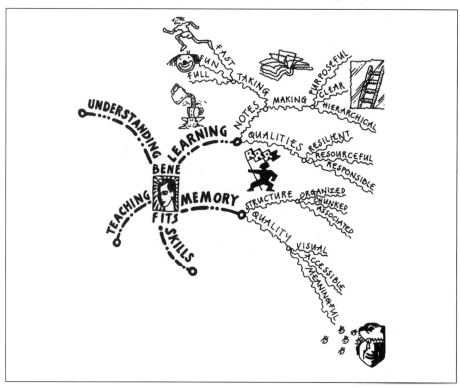

that, unlike linear text, the information is always **accessible** and it is easy to add or show relationships. The final quality that we chose to emphasize was the **meaningful** nature of maps. Because the learner can see relationships between the parts and the whole all at the same time, and because she has had to organize the information, she creates some kind of meaning for herself.

The "learning" branch

9.   Because we made the earlier decision of creating separate branches for "memory", "understanding" and "skills", we discussed what other benefits we could highlight for "learners". We decided to map the **qualities** that mapping promotes in learners and to emphasize that model mapping is a very effective method for making and taking **notes**.

10. Our experience of working with students in school is that once learners know how they learn they become more **resilient** – it's as if they "know that they can know" so they are less likely to "give up". Learners with mapping skills are therefore far more **resourceful** and able to take more **responsibility** for forging meaning and understanding for themselves. (Along with "resilience", these qualities make up the "three Rs".)

11. Using mapping to take notes while listening to a speaker supports the learner, and helps to make the experience less like dictation followed by handwriting exercise. The notes become **full** as the learner is supported in seeing and making connections. Because keywords or concepts are identified, the process is **fast**. Because thinking is visually supported the act becomes more **fun**. The demand for structure that is inherent in mapping makes note-making more **purposeful**. The learner can see how their notes are **hierarchical** in nature. They are supported in making their thinking **clear**.

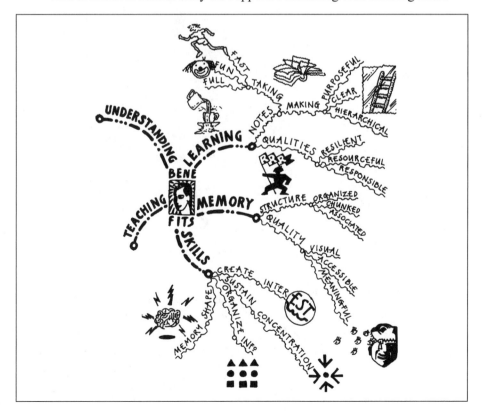

The "skills" branch

12. As a learner learns he displays certain skills. During the learning process, the learner must be **interested**, able to **concentrate**, **organize information** and **memorize** the work. This entire section is very closely associated with the rest of the map: there is a whole branch on "memory", "organizing information" is directly linked to the "understanding" branch and "interest" and "concentration" are a direct consequence of the "three Rs" found in the "learning" branch. Mapping contributes directly to the development of these skills.

The "teaching" branch

13. We discussed how we could show succinctly that mapping has impact in all areas of a teacher's work. We decided to use the "**plan-do-review**" model since we felt teachers would recognize this without further explanation.

14. Using mapping to plan work, meetings or presentations is **fast**. You have an **overview** available to you at any time and, as explained in chapter 7, it is a great way to make planning a more **creative** experience.

   In chapters 6 and 7 you will see the impact that mapping can have on **flexible** and **ordered** classroom delivery. You will also find out how mapping can be used to gauge students' **understanding** of your delivery and why it is such a powerful **memory** technique.

The "understanding" branch

15. We believe that teaching and learning is all about helping the learner to understand. We wanted to emphasize this, so we gave understanding a branch of its own. We then discussed how a map promoted understanding and we decided to map the three main ways.

    Without a map, learning is like trying to do a jigsaw puzzle without the lid of the box. Learners need to see how the individual pieces fit into the whole – the **big picture**. It is also clear that you cannot understand something unless you **organize the information** in such a way that it makes sense to you. Using maps also enables you to see **connections** between different areas of the map. As the map below shows, there are many connections to be made between the individual elements.

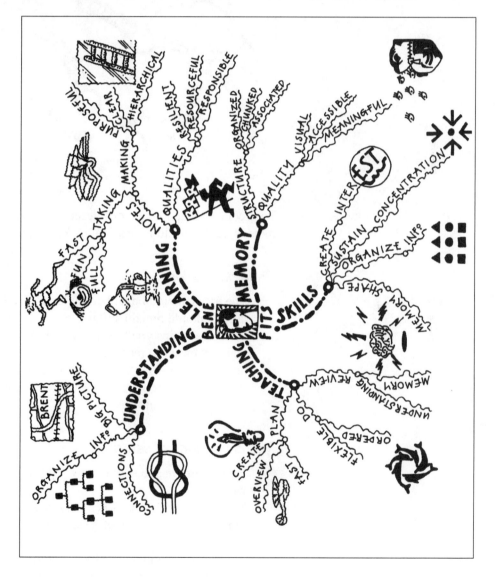

Key rules to follow when mapping

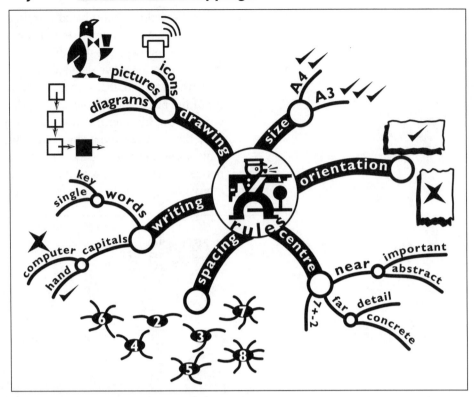

To produce a map like the one described above, there are a small number of rules or guidelines to follow that make the job easier for you.

Page orientation

- The paper should be laid out in landscape format (this is, wider than it is tall). It should remain still while you are mapping. Keeping the paper horizontal helps you to keep your writing and drawings horizontal. This makes it easier to read and comprehend when complete, because you do not have to move it to look at any particular aspect. In turn, this aids memory since your peripheral vision is able to take in the whole of the map, the whole of the time.

The importance of centre

- Your centre image and/or keyword should be something that represents the whole.
- You should only have 7 (±2) key ideas coming from the centre, as you can remember a maximum of 7 (±2) ideas readily. (See Earth in Space map on page 108.)
- The words around the centre will normally be abstract and generalized in nature and be of greater importance than those further away from the centre. The words towards the outside of the map will be more concrete or specific in nature but less important to the overall structure of the model map. Having 7 (±2) key abstract words at the centre provides a platform for the rest of the map to build upon, since they, if chosen correctly, will

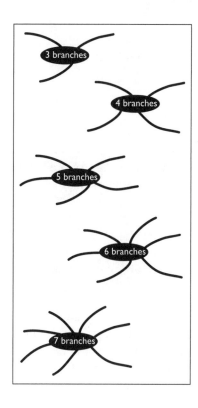

have a large potential to "capture" subordinate ideas. (See Combatting Bullying map on page 109.)

Spacing

- The number of branches you have coming from the centre will affect the use of space on the paper. After mapping for a while you develop an ability to predict the space you will need for each branch.
- The branches should be spread evenly around the centre and the branches kept as horizontal as possible at all times. The areas to the left and right of centre are easiest to map on; the areas above and below centre are the hardest. Look at the maps at the start of each chapter, and the diagrams to the left which model ideal spacing.
- White space is important as it provides borders for the words and images on your map. It helps them to stand out and therefore helps you to remember them. It also represents the space in which additional ideas, and explanations of the relationships between the key concepts, can – and do – show up.

Writing

- Use single words wherever possible. This makes additional associations easier.
- As we saw earlier, nouns carry most meanings and associations. Use them as much as possible rather than verbs, adjectives and so on.
- Use capital letters: they are easier to read, tend to be neater and are therefore easier to commit to memory (unless of course your small case writing is particularly neat, in which case use whatever you feel most comfortable with).
- You can give words at the centre added emphasis by making them bolder and bigger then those towards the periphery.

Using icons, pictures and graphic images

- Icons, pictures and graphic images can be used to replace many words and/or to summarize whole sections of a map. Just as a noun will stimulate more associations in your memory than a verb, so an image can stimulate a whole series of thoughts and memories. When we think of a noun we automatically see an image of it in our mind's eye, but when we see a picture or image it stimulates more of our sense than a single word. (See Earth in Space and Mapping: Methodology and Applications map on pages 108 and 113.)

Size of paper

- You can map onto any size of paper. The authors send post cards that are mapped!

Step-by-step guide to mapping

The following sections will present three versions of mapping possibilities:

- Dump it, organize it, map it
- The book analogy
- The literal approach

These guides to mapping will certainly be of most practical benefit if you consider a topic related to work-in-progress that could usefully be explored and studied through mapping. Decide how each of these three versions fit your content and which fits best.

Dump it, organize it, map it (DOM)

To carry out the following steps, you will need three or four sheets of blank paper.

1. Think of a central word, theme or area of interest that you would like to produce a map on. Write this word in the middle of the page, which you have arranged in a landscape fashion, and draw a boundary around it.
2. Keeping the page horizontal, draw lines or branches out from the centre, and on these lines write single words that you associate with the central image or theme. Remember, write only one word per line. If you think of a word that is more closely associated with the word on the line than with the word in the centre, draw a line off this "radiating" word and write the new word on this line. Similarly, this word may have associations of its own. If so, draw another line branching off it, and so on. Write down any words that "spring to mind" – try not to select or "get it right". Keep doing this until the central image is surrounded by associations. (Aim for 15 to 20.)
3. If you can, find someone to read and explain your associated words to. Explain why you have made those associations. Move your finger over the paper as you do so. If you are working alone, talk through your associations to yourself. Add any new words you think of.
   This is not, as you now know, a map. What you have is a series of words that you freely associated with your central idea. You will now start organizing your ideas into a map.
4. Look at the words you have written on the page. See if you can find words that go together.
5. Look at your groupings of words. What word would you use to describe each group? In effect you are identifying the organizing principle for the group. Put another way, you are looking for the main headings of your map. The "organizing principle" word may or may not already be written down. Try to find enough organizing principles to encompass all of the words you have generated.
6. Using a clean sheet of paper, redraw your central idea and add the organizing principles that you have established around it.
7. Now add the words that you originally brainstormed to the relevant branches on your map.
8. Add any other additional words that you think of as they occur to you.

9. Now either go to page 55 (**Developing your maps**), or spend some time practicing your new skill. Alternatively, you could read and try out the other two step-by-step guides given below.

The book analogy

In this method we are going to use an analogy: pretend that the topic you have chosen to map is going to be written up as a book. (Alternatively, for practice, you could map a book you know well.)

1. Think of a title for the book and/or a main image to represent the book. This is the centre of your map.
2. Now think what the chapter headings in your book might be. Think carefully before deciding what the chapters are going to be about. Ask yourself questions such as:

    - Would this chapter title be part of the bigger chapter?
    - If so what should this bigger chapter be called?

    In effect, you are "revising" ideas about language triangles from earlier in this chapter (page 30).

    Once you have chosen your chapter headings, draw branches out from the centre (remember the advice on page 51 regarding spacing, though with practice you will learn to judge the space you need for each branch). Write the words you have chosen to represent your chapters along these lines.
3. Relate to each of your main branches or "chapter headings" as if it were a book in itself. What would be the main sub-sections of each? Once you have decided on keywords to represent these sub-sections, draw smaller branches off each of the main ones and add the keywords. Remember an image or diagram can be used at any time instead of a word.

    You now have the title of the book (the centre of the map), the chapter headings (the main branches) and the sections within each of the chapters (the smaller branches off the main ones).

    You may have noticed how each branch exists within, and is enveloped by, the previous one. You may have realized how the work so far in this chapter has been preparing you for this. If you have not read fully the first sections of this chapter, and are finding this difficult to follow, try going back and completing the reading and exercises on page 27 to 44.
4. Further branches can be added to each of the "sub-heading" branches, and seen as paragraph headings within the sub-headings, within the chapter headings, within the book.
5. Now either go to page 55 (**Developing your maps**), or spend some time practicing your new skill. Alternatively, you could read and try out the other two step-by-step guides given above and on page 54.

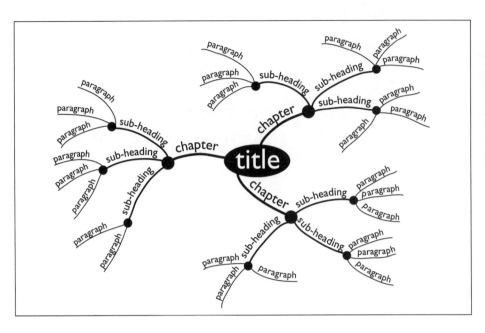

The literal approach

1. Draw a picture or icon representing the subject of the map. Alternatively, you could use a strong image created with letters, perhaps using drop shadows, unusual typefaces, and so on. Use color if possible.
2. Decide what are the main categories of information. There will be between 5 and 9 of these main ideas. They are organizing principles of your map and may be the most abstract words you use.
3. Use a keyword to "summarize" each of these main ideas or overarching categories.
4. Take one of these main ideas; estimate how long the keyword will be if written in large letters, and then draw a "branch" of that length from the central image. Use a chosen color. Now, write the keyword just above the line, in capital letters in the same color as the line. All subsequent and subordinate keywords, lines, illustrations and icons should be in that color.
5. Concentrating on this one main category, consider what sub-categories you want within it. For each of these, think of a keyword that best and memorably summarizes the sub-category. Again, estimate the length of line needed to accommodate the keyword, and draw it in a way that shows it is of less significance than the main idea. You can do this by estimating its length when the keyword is written in a smaller size than the main keyword. You can also emphasize its subordinate value to the main branch by drawing a thinner, less ornate line.
6. Repeat this process for all the first level of sub-categories until all the information you wanted to map has been given a keyword and "place".
7. Now, look over this whole branch and see if all the keywords are appropriately categorized. The physical placement is a very visual and spatial way of checking this.
8. See if there are any links you want to emphasize by drawing arrows from keyword(s) to keyword(s). These links may illustrate a relationship not apparent within the hierarchy of categories used.

9. You can now repeat the whole process for each of the other main organizing keyword branches.

10. You can deviate from the above sequence, and indeed it's a good idea to do so. These instructions have been written in a linear, sequential way shaping a linear, sequential response from you. This is only needed for your first few maps, as you become familiar with the logic of categories and sub-categories. Once you feel secure in this and the graphic rules used to present them, you are free to deviate – to jump from one spot to any other spot of the map. Simply write down the ideas and keywords as you think of them.

    So, if you are struggling or stuck on one branch and an idea pops up about another branch, do not bother to store it for later – use it immediately. This gives you the sense of working "with the brain", not harnessing it to an unnatural, linear and sequential process. However, you need to master the logic of categories initially. When you do, you will be able to benefit from the power of being both creative and organized.

11. When you have finished, scan your map, looking for sense in the categories and completeness in the details of the outer minor branches. Travel along the branches to test out the logic of the ride.

12. Add to, cross out and redraw your map if needed.

13. Explain your map to someone else, both to check out your understanding and to lock the map into your memory.

Developing your maps

Review the work that you completed in the previous sections. Which versions worked best for your topic, content and purpose? As you review the following information about developing your maps, think about your use of color, size, icons, diagrams and pictures in your own map.

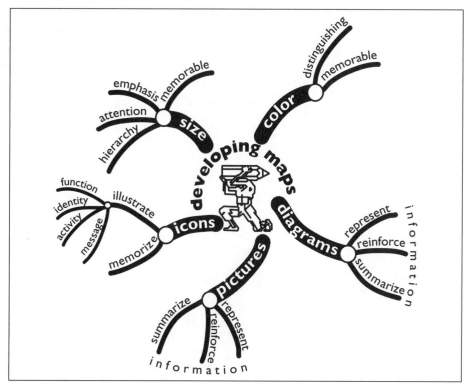

Until now we have concentrated on using words. In fact, we have concentrated on the skill of categorization and have used words to illustrate the thinking and methodology. You may have already thought about ways in which you can make your maps more unique, memorable and personal. This may aid recall and add interest for yourself as a learner.

Use of color
Using a different color for each of the main branches makes them more distinct from one another and aids the recall of information. The use of color can make images, icons and diagrams stand out from the background.

Use of size
Size can provide emphasis. The most important branches and words at the centre could be larger than those towards the outside. Attention tends to be drawn to the largest words first. These initial branches are the organizing principles of a map and encompass the information contained further away.

Use of icons
Icons can be used to summarize a number of words or to indicate a function or activity. They can convey a message and provide something with a unique identity. An icon can convey or carry more information than a single keyword and because of its form can be more readily remembered. You can collect icons, borrow icons and make up your own.

Use of diagrams
Diagrams are used to provide a visual representation of a significant amount of information. Diagrams can be used to illustrate the workings of something or to summarize the results. Examples of diagrams include bar, flow and pie charts, Venn diagrams and maps!

Use of pictures
Like diagrams and icons, pictures can be used to represent, reinforce and summarize significant amounts of information. You do not need to be good at drawing to include pictures in your maps. You do need to be clear about what the picture represents to you. The size of the picture should depend on its importance and therefore its location with respect to the centre.

Teaching mapping

changing linear learners into holographic thinkers

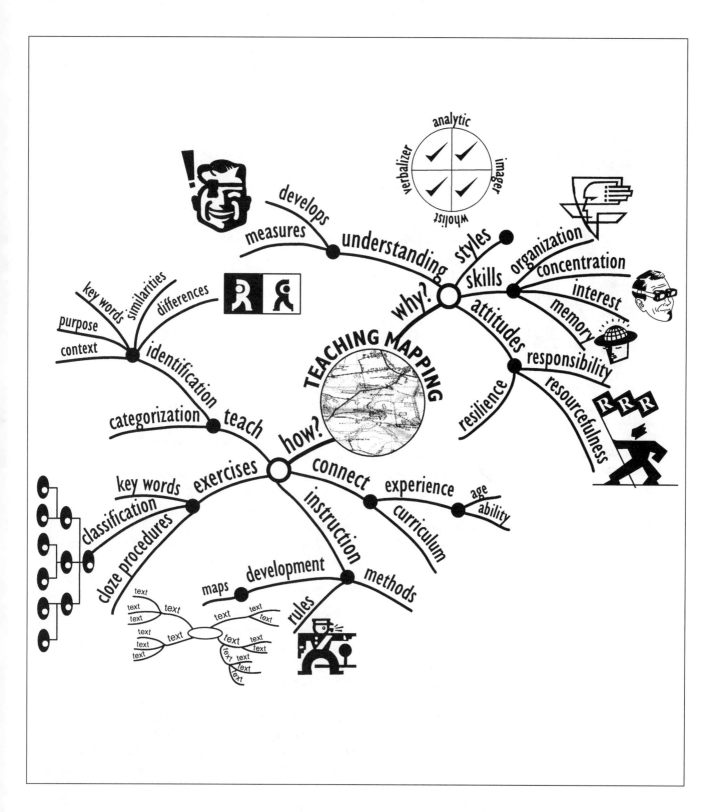

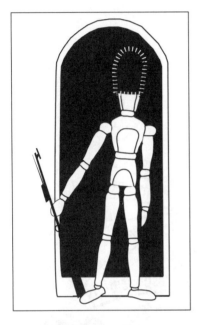

Ian remembers a very early example of someone trying to show him how to read and use a map. This is his story. "I remember, aged 6 or 7, being taken to London to see Buckingham Palace. My Auntie Rhoda tried to teach me how to read the London underground maps. I could understand the ones in the trains above the seats, the ones with only one color and one line; I enjoyed "guessing" which station was coming next and grinned when my guess proved correct. But try as I (and she) might, I could not make head nor tail of the multi-colored, multi-dimensional maps that showed how all the bits went together. It was 15 years before I next went on the underground and I remember two things about this: first, my anxiety about going on the underground without my Auntie Rhoda to show me how to get from London Bridge to Richmond; second, my relief when I realized that I could read and make sense of the big complicated maps by myself – it was easy."

Sometimes realizing how easy something is can be really hard and can take a long time.

What follows in this chapter is not, of course, the only way to introduce and teach model mapping to learners. But, having read it, you should certainly be more successful than Ian's Auntie Rhoda at teaching students to think holographically. If this chapter, and indeed the rest of the book, stimulates your own ideas (and perhaps gets more students using public transport!) then it will have fulfilled a wider purpose.

This chapter is divided into two sections:

- Why teach mapping?
- How to teach mapping

Why teach mapping?

It is important to realize that in teaching students to produce maps you are not merely teaching them another "study skill" or a "memory tool" to help them recall information for the next test or examination – although mapping does fulfil these functions. You are making available to them something that will support them in creating meaning and hence understanding for themselves, wherever and whenever they choose to do so, for the rest of their lives.

The learning experience is the responsibility of the learner; it takes place in the learner. By teaching students to map, you are supporting them in taking responsibility for their own learning. You are showing them how they can and do create meaning in the world. It is a gift. It is up to them if they choose to use it. It is up to us as educators to show them what it can make available to them as learners.

In school students are asked to listen to, explore, make sense of and understand the thinking structures and knowledge associated with many different subjects. They are presented with different models of thinking each day. As they move between subjects, they experience the thinking, knowledge and concepts (or at least the teacher's interpretation of the concepts) of each one, which can be very different in nature to the last. In order to understand each subject, students must switch from one way of thinking to another as they move through the school day. Having been exposed to these different stimuli, students are then asked to demonstrate their understanding via essays, tests, comprehension exercises and the like; the standard of work that results can be extremely variable.

Written or spoken messages are necessarily linear sequences of concepts and propositions. In contrast, knowledge is stored in our minds in a kind of hierarchical or holographic structure. When we generate written or spoken sentences, we must transform information from a hierarchical to a linear structure. Conversely, when we read or hear messages, we must transform linear sequences into a hierarchical structure in order to assimilate them into our minds. Concept mapping can aid this psychological–linguistic transformation.

J. D. Novak and *D. B. Gowin*

Gifted students tend to do this reorganization on their own, but even they will profit from learning more systematic approaches to organizing knowledge, especially ways to see better its hierarchical structure. Less talented students usually resort to rote learning as the only alternative that allows them to maintain their self-esteem in the face of an otherwise almost hopeless learning task. Less motivated students simply give up and become behavior problems or engage in what Holt (1964) called "strategies for failure".

J. D. Novak and *D. B. Gowin*

…[education] needs to emphasize the skills of devising and assessing constructs and techniques, the skills of thinking.

G. A. Woditsch

The essays and answers that the teacher receives are a physical representation of a student's ability to take in, organize, make sense of, and then reorganize into linear fashion, the stimulus that has been provided. Students are not necessarily aware of how they have carried out this process, and this is the point. By teaching students to map you can show them how they make sense of the world by organizing information. Once revealed, this new-found knowledge can be used by your students to organize all future information that comes their way. Unless students know how they make sense of the world – unless this subconscious skill is made evident and available – the standard of work that they produce cannot be regarded in any way as their best.

Mapping is important because it allows and encourages students to:

- analyze and make connections
- become better thinkers
- learn meaningfully
- think flexibly
- communicate effectively
- become active creators of their own knowledge and frameworks of interpretation
- search out meaning and impose structure
- go beyond the information given
- deal systematically yet flexibly with novel problems and situations
- adopt a critical attitude to information and argument
- make reasoned judgements
- make their own thought processes more explicit.

See Mapping: Methodology and Applications map on page 113.

The real question, it seems, is not "Why do it?", but "What possible reason could anybody have for not teaching children to understand and use mapping in their learning and in life?"

How to teach mapping

This section is divided up under the following headings:

- Connecting the learning
- Exercises: identifying keywords
- Exercises: keywords and language hierarchies
- Exercises: organizing information
- Exercises: from linear to holographic thinking
- Drawing their own map

Connecting the learning

In this important first section, students learn that maps are useful, and are introduced to the vocabulary and processes that they will need in developing their mapping skills. The section examines:

- Student reactions to mapping
- Linking to experience: introducing keywords, selection and organization
- Internalization of maps.

What follows is intended to inform the way you teach model mapping to your students, though it is not a step-by-step approach that has to be followed in a strict way.

Student reactions to mapping

…students need explicit guidance in learning about learning and in the tools and strategies to facilitate meaningful learning.

Joseph Novak

Unsurprisingly, students react differently to mapping depending, in part, on their age and experience of schools to date.

The good news is that the authors have yet to work with any students – from international MBA students to children with severe, emotional or behavioral learning difficulties – who did not see the value of mapping in the end. Generally speaking, the older the students, the more difficult they can find it to "give up" established working practices for new methods. A grade 12 student once said he found it hard getting used to the idea that he did not have to write lots of (linear) notes in order to learn. He added that he felt comfortable writing down lots of stuff. When asked if this helped him learn, he said "I don't know, it just feels comforting and I feel as if I have done a lot".

Other students may find it hard to accept that fewer notes and less writing does not mean "harder to learn or remember". There are many variations of this concern, probably associated with students' experience of working in a linear fashion for a significant period of time. Put simply, the older they are the more initial resistance there may be.

Whatever their age, students will normally be pleased to hear how to spend less time on homework and get better results, so start by focusing on the "pupil payoff". Going into the classroom and declaring that "today we are going to learn a new way of learning called mapping" and then getting straight down to exercises will be pretty meaningless, and therefore may well meet with a mixed reaction!

You may choose to introduce mapping to your students by creating a map on the board as you teach a lesson. Or, you can walk students through a map of your own or one of the maps from the Gallery of maps. (See Mapping: Methodology and Application on page 113.)

Linking to experience: introducing keywords, selection and organization

For all students, try to connect the idea of learning how to map with their own direct experience of maps. With adults and teenage students, look at and discuss maps that are familiar; maps of the locality, road maps or survey maps, for example. With younger children, try studying maps of the school or of adventure theme parks.

Try to draw out specific insights that will be mirrored when you start mapping. These insights are described below.

- **Selection of information**
  Information has been selected for the purpose for which the map was designed. Develop the idea of selection by looking at what is not on the map; discuss what things could have been included and possible reasons why they were not.
- **Keywords and symbols**
  Individual keywords and symbols on the map are used to convey messages, themes and ideas that, once known, carry associations. Explore the use of the information key to develop and illustrate the idea.

- **Graphical organization**

  How useful would a map be if it listed the place names but did not show graphically their positions relative to one another? How easy would it be to set out, and to use, the same information in linear form?

  Expand on the idea of presentation by looking at the use of font, color, type size and spacing, and the effect this has on the reader in terms of providing emphasis and distinction of different areas, functions and purposes.

- **Maps are useful**

  Discuss the advantages that someone with a map has over someone without one. In general terms, discuss the emphasis that has been given to certain pieces of information on the map, how this emphasis has been given and what the purpose of the map is. Ask why the map has the boundaries it has, and what other maps it might be contained within.

  Most importantly, try to develop a sense that maps are useful, and that (assuming we know how to use them) they give us confidence.

- **Make a map**

  After spending some time looking at and discussing maps, give students the opportunity to create a map themselves for a specific purpose, to reinforce and demonstrate the learning.

  Older students or adults might create a map giving directions to a party. Younger students could create a map to help a new student find his way around school or the classroom. In each case, the learner is asked to do two things: first, to select the information needed to fulfil the purpose of the map; second, to organize the information so that it is useful. Spend time emphasizing these points: that the information chosen is a selection of the total available, and that it only becomes useful once it has been organized.

Internalization of maps

We all have memorized maps of places that we are familiar with. The students, for example, have all memorized how to find their way around their classrooms, their homes, their school, the locality and so on. When we go on vacation, we spend the first few hours (or days!) "getting our bearings" – finding out where things are in relation to everything else.

With older learners, you could talk about how a particular car journey may initially require a physical map. This map gets internalized, eventually, and we soon do the journey automatically (until one day, the road is closed and we have to find an alternative route).

Both a physical map and an internalized one are useful. The ability to read and use them gives us confidence. Ask the learners for examples of other maps that they have internalized. List them on the board, and show that we all use them all of the time. Without them we couldn't find or do very much at all.

Exercises: identifying keywords

We have already introduced the idea that information on maps is selected. Now we want to show how most of the meaning is carried in a very small number of keywords.

The following exercises are intended to give you some ideas and initial ways of demonstrating and teaching this to your students. Some of the exercises themselves will be familiar from chapter 2; here, though, they are set out to show how they may be delivered in a classroom situation.

Exercise 1

Ask students to complete Worksheet 1: using keywords in writing on page 27 to recall a recent trip or vacation.

To help get the students started, provide sentence stems or writing frames detailing the types of things that they could write about. For example, they could write about the location, weather, people, travel arrangements, feelings, thoughts, funniest/best/worst/scariest moments.

When it is obvious to you that they would be unable to get even a quarter of their information onto a postcard, ask the students to stop writing. Hand out postcard-sized pieces of blank paper, and ask them to write all of their information about the trip on it. When they protest that it is impossible, ask them to put their writing to one side and move on to the next exercise.

Exercise 2

Write a sentence up on the board, omitting the nouns, verbs and adjectives. Ask the class to guess what the sentence is about as you write it. Now add the adjectives, and let them guess again. Next, add the verbs, and let them guess. Finally, add the nouns. This is a very easy way to demonstrate that nouns carry most meaning. (The language you use in talking about this exercise will depend on the students' familiarity with the terms "noun", "verb" and "adjective".)

Ask the students which words they could actually draw. One of the reasons that nouns are easier to recall is because we can "see" them as well as say them. Adjectives and verbs can only be seen in terms of their relationship to the noun. So, in recalling the noun you are likely to recall the verb and adjective too.

If appropriate for your class, you may choose to have your students also complete Worksheet 2: the importance of nouns on page 28.

Exercise 3

Have your students return to their writing about their trip (Worksheet 1: using keywords in writing on page 27) by asking them to complete Worksheet 3: postcard map on page 29.

Exercises: keywords and language hierarchies

You may find it useful to revisit the section on language hierarchies in chapter 2 (page 30).

Seeing that words can be placed within language hierarchies will help your students select the words that they need for their maps. The following exercises are designed to help you teach your students that language exists in hierarchies. You will be developing their ability to see higher and lower order relationships between words. In essence, the following exercises contain within them all the skills needed to be a proficient mapper. They are skills we all have to varying degrees. What you will be doing is making them obvious to the students.

It is tempting when you start mapping to think that you need to use lots of keywords in order to record, and therefore remember, information – you don't. The exercises below are designed to help students see how best to select

Data are facts; information is the meaning that human beings assign to these facts. Individual elements of data, by themselves, have little meaning; it's only when these facts are in some way put together or processed that the meaning begins to become clear.

William S. Davis and
Allison McCormack

keywords by "seeing" and using language "triangles". (See Medal Collecting map on page 107.)

Exercise 1

Ask students to complete Worksheet 4: creating language triangles on page 33.

As a class, discuss their responses. Then, use other groups of words to explore categorization; see if the students can make up some of their own using their favorite topics. For example, ask them to list favorite TV characters, computer games or personalities (TV characters could be a sub-group of favorite personalities). Then ask them to divide the list up into groups or categories. Computer games could be divided up by type, or by manufacturer. TV characters could be grouped into male or female. Ask the students to come up with their own ways of categorizing their lists.

When using maps as an active learning tool in the classroom you will see how it is always vital to keep asking "Is this keyword part of a bigger group?", and "What words are contained within or under this one?". (See Medal Collecting map on page 107.) Students can start to practise using these questions as they classify and categorize their lists of words.

Exercise 2

Have students complete Worksheet 5: using language triangles to map on page 34. In this exercise, a brainstormed list of words associated with a central theme is gradually categorized and placed in language "triangles" or hierarchies, to form a map. (You may want students to do this exercise after they have completed the next section on "organizing information".)

Exercises: organizing information

This section is divided up into the following areas:

- Organizing principles around us
- Exercises

Organizing principles around us

The child recalls a sequence of heaps. She notes likenesses across that sequence. She joins those likenesses in a new representation of experience, a representation more durable and wieldy because it leaves out extraneous sense data. She has formed a complex.

G. A. Woditsch

When working with learners of all ages, spend a little time exploring what it would be like if things were not organized. Discuss and identify examples of organizing principles around us. Talk about how the organization of shops makes our lives easier. Discuss examples of organization at home; for example, how clothes, food, books and so on are arranged. Schools are very organized places too. For example, most secondary schools have space organized by function and by subject or department. Primary classrooms often have specific areas allocated for specific purposes; these "stations" are also organized by function. Even teachers' cupboards and students' bedrooms have some degree of organization!

Exercises

While these exercises may appear self-explanatory, it is a mistake to assume that everyone will find them easy; even the most able students may find them challenging. Enjoy watching your students learn how they learn. Following the exercises, invite students to talk about and complete journal entries about what they learned about themselves as learners.

Organization of lizards

On Worksheet 6 on page 36, are four lizards, labelled a, b, c, d. Point out to the students that these represent units of information that need organizing. Ask students to do parts 1 and 2 of the exercise to indicate how they could be organized, first according to size and second by color. Then ask them to complete part 3 to show how they could be organized by size and color.

With the students, try to think of real life examples where objects are organized by size, color or both.

Organization of monsters

On Worksheet 7 on page 37 are four monsters labelled a, b, c, d. Support the students in following the instructions to complete parts 1, 2, 3 and 4.

Organization of geometric shapes

The series of tasks shown on Worksheet 8 on page 38 uses geometric shapes as an analogy for information. There are a number of different shapes of different sizes and colors. At present they are not organized or classified in any way.

At this point, emphasize that everything is connected to something else in order for a meaning to be made. Part 1 of this exercise asks students to collect their data. Part 2 asks them to establish the possible principles of classification that they could use to organize the shapes. Part 3 asks them to classify the shapes according to shape, color and size. Explain the nature of the exercise, and then support the students as they work through each part.

Developing classification skills

The following exercise, which is a variation on those above, is designed to show students that the same information can be classified in different ways depending on the purpose and context.

The heads on Worksheet 14 on page 67 differ in a number of ways – in size, in "expression", in shape, in the presence or absence of a hat or beard or glasses and so on. Have students complete the exercise and then share how they classified the heads.

Ask students to make up their own selection of different heads or faces, in groups. Then ask them to swap with another group and to classify the selection they are given.

Exercises: from linear to holographic thinking

By the end of this section, students will have practised using their organization skills and will have experienced for themselves the fact that a map is nothing more than a series of key concepts organized hierarchically around a central point. Students will see for themselves that more information can be put down onto paper when organized in this way than through using linear notes. Most importantly, perhaps, by the end of this section students will actually be drawing maps as opposed to writing in linear form.

The cloze procedure exercises described below (see pages 40–44) revisit work done to date and give the learner the confidence needed to move forwards.

We have taught classification skills by setting up a role play in which a bouncer on the door at a night-club either refuses or allows entry depending on various criteria, such as style of clothes or shoes. Once in the club, we examined other examples of classification – drinks, music, "types" or people (age groups, dress codes). A lot of PSHE, Maths and English work came out of this initial fun role play.

Oliver Caviglioli

Taking students through classification

Ask students to look at the mapping classification of a shoe shop on page 39.

At the top is shown one possible classification tree for a shoe shop. The main classification of the stock is by intended wearer – the shoes are divided up under "male", "female" and "children". Beneath the classification "male" the shoes are classified into "types"; namely "sports", "casual", and "dress". (The same classification could have been used for "female" and "children", but for the purpose of the exercise only the "male" shoes have been classified.) The classification tree goes on to show the organization of the shoes according to color and size.

Below the tree is a map of the same information. The subject of the classification, "shoes", is at the centre and the main organizing or classification principles – namely "male", "female" and "children" – radiate from the centre. The organizing principles of male shoes – "sports", "casual" and "dress" – then branch off from "male". Point out to the students that there is room to classify the "female" and "children" shoes in the same way here if required, whereas there was little space in the classification tree. Make sure they understand that this is the *same* information represented in a different way.

Ultimately this is what a map is: a series of key ideas or principles stemming from, and classified around, a central theme or idea. Do not assume that all students will see this automatically; they may not. You are their guide – "walk and talk" them through the exercises.

Lead the students through the exercises shown on pages 40 – 44 (Worksheets 9 – 13); they will find other information that has been classified and represented in a map. Ask them to copy out each map onto a blank sheet of paper. In each subsequent exercise, they will see that more and more information has been omitted from the map. Their job is to fill in the gaps.

As they work through the maps, make sure that they are thinking ahead and check that they are transferring information to the right areas. Ask them how else the information could have been organized.

Drawing their own map

Most students will be ready to start drawing their own maps after completing the classification exercises above. Give them the opportunity to produce their own map independently. You could give the whole class the same topic or let them choose. A good map to start with is one about each student. (See Me! maps on pages 104–106. These maps were created by students about themselves.) These maps can include all kinds of information: favourite meals, activities, interests, sports, friends, school or pets. To get students started, you could post the framework on page 66.

Before students begin their maps, you may wish to:

* Review the "rules of mapping" with students (page 50). Alternatively you could map these rules onto a board for them to refer to as they draw.
* Let each student draw a map independently, or take them through the process using one of the step-by-step guides on pages 52 to 55.
* Model the ways that students can develop their maps using pictures, icons, color, and so on (page 56).

- Photocopy and post several examples of maps from the Gallery of Maps around the room for students to use as models. (See Nutrition on page 100, First Aid on page 101 or Medal Collecting on page 107.)

As they draw their maps, circulate and make a mental note of which students have "got it" and which students need further support.

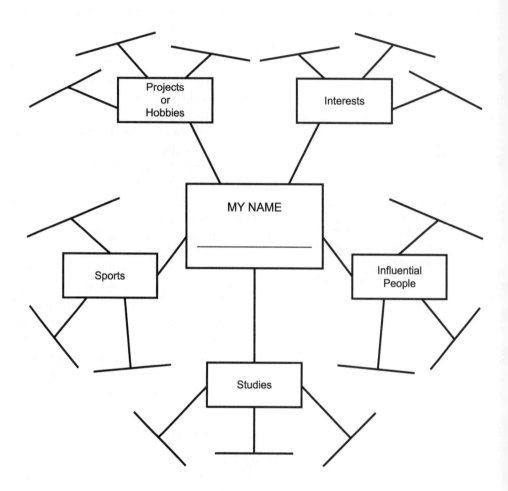

Name: _____

Worksheet 14: classifying information

The heads below differ in a number of ways — in size, "expression", shape and so on. Cut these heads into cards and sort them into groups. Be prepared to explain how you classified the heads.

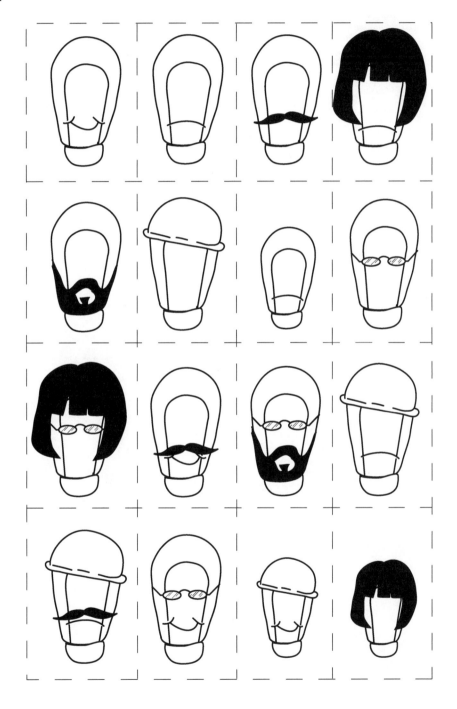

4 Thinking skills

developing thinking skills through mapping

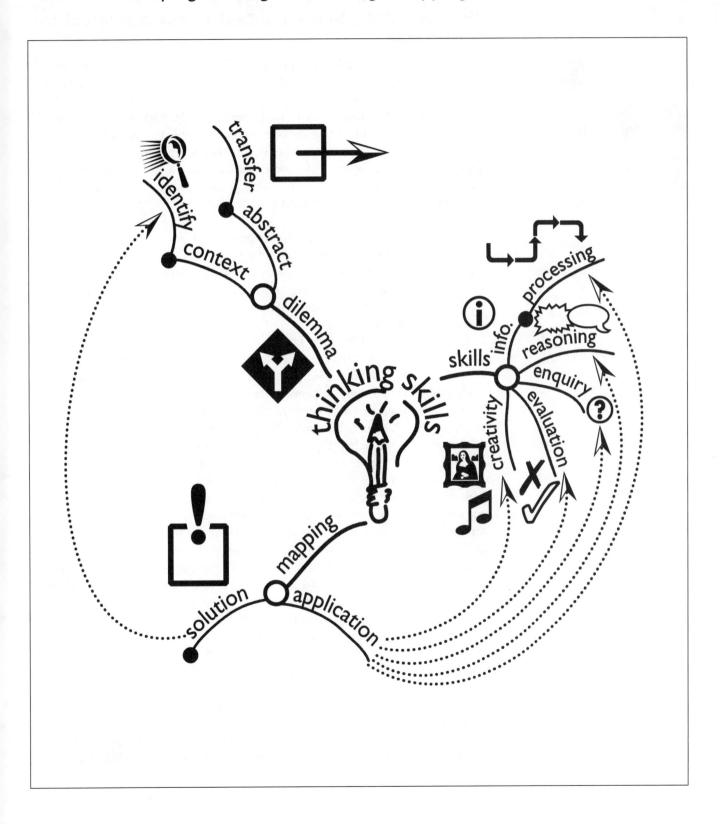

69

This chapter is divided up into two sections:

- Thinking skills in the context of subject-specific instruction
- Mapping as a strategy for subject-specific thinking

Thinking skills in the context of subject-specific instruction

The teaching of thinking is a real problem. We all value the development of this faculty in our students; we are not clear, however, on the best way to go about making sure it develops.

There are various thinking skills programmes on the market. Their authors claim that students completing the courses are then able to use their newly developed skills in any area they choose. In other words, the students are able to apply the *general* thinking skills learned in the course to *specific* subjects. Unfortunately, the evidence does not support such claims – there seems to be a real problem in transferring abstract and generalized thinking skills to be used effectively in specific contexts.

Mapping provides one solution to the problem of how you can embed thinking skills into subject knowledge. Since the mid 1970s, the benefits of mapping have been almost entirely focused on its brain-friendly processes and its capacity for creativity. However, perhaps even greater benefit lies in the way the analytical and organizational skills needed to map in turn lead to the development of thinking skills.

Thinking does not take place in a vacuum. You cannot separate the context of your subject from the "thinking of your subject". Each particular subject has a way of thinking and this thinking is shaped by the language of the subject.

One of the premier philosophers of the twentieth century, Ludwig Wittgenstein, proposed that there are "forms of life' and that these domains of existence have their own particular "language games". Furthermore, he asserted, all thought is based in language. These different forms of life, having their own language games, consequently produce different types of thinking. As McPeck concludes " ... there are almost as many distinguishable logics, or kinds of reasoning, as there are distinguishable kinds of subjects". In other words, your subject area has its own language and thinking skills. In order to improve the thinking skills of your students, you need to improve their knowledge of and use of the language associated with the discipline.

Another philosopher, Postman, makes this remarkably clear when he says: "As one learns the language of a subject, one is also learning what that subject is. It cannot be said often enough that what we call a subject consists mostly, if not entirely, of its language. If you eliminate all the words of a subject, you have eliminated the subject. Biology is not plants and animals. It is language about plants and animals. History is not events. It is language describing and interpreting events. Astronomy is not planets and stars. It is a way of talking about planets and stars."

The specialized language of a subject is the key to the development of subject-specific thinking. As leading curriculum designer Jerome Bruner pointed out decades ago, subjects have key concepts, which are the building blocks of our ability to talk about the subject, and to make distinctions and form links and relationships within it.

Let [a subject] be taught in such a way that the student learns what substantive structures gave rise to the chosen body of knowledge, what the strengths and weaknesses of these structures are and what some of the alternatives are which give rise to alternative bodies of knowledge.

J.J. Schwab

We do not think in a linear, sequential way, yet every body of information is given to us in a linear manner. Even language structure is basically linear ... we are taught to communicate in a way that is actually restricting our ability to think, because we think in an associative way. When we read a sentence we do not limit our intake of information to what we see in that sentence. We actually make innumerable associations with our own experience. We read in ways we do not write.

Peter Bradford

As a teacher, the language and key concepts of your subject are very familiar and comfortable to you. Clearly, however, there has been no opportunity for teachers in general to make these subject-specific thought structures and rules explicit – hence the appearance of thinking skills programmes "by default". As the next section explains, mapping can play a key role in making this subject-specific language and thinking available – and, indeed, teachable by all teachers to all students.

Since thinking skills are developed within specific subjects, it follows that it is the responsibility of the subject teacher to teach thinking skills. The advantage of this approach is that the teaching of thinking skills will not be a "bolt on" task since each teacher will be "on their own turf". Teachers are asked to take on an extra dimension of their chosen discipline, and consequently, it is hoped, subject teaching will improve and standards will be raised.

This now begs the question of how exactly teachers are to accomplish this. How can you make explicit, in a variety of modalities, the basic structure from which your descriptions and explanations originate? How can teachers "give away" their organizing principles? How can they communicate their grasp of their subject, which makes their consequent understanding and retention of information so easy and invisible? This is the pedagogical problem that must be addressed if we are to resolve the apparent division between developing thinking skills and subject teaching.

Mapping as a strategy for subject-specific thinking

Before you can produce a map you need to be able to do two things. First, you need the knowledge and skills of mapping. Second, you need a knowledge and an understanding of the content to be mapped.

Chapter 2 provides exercises that make the strategies and skills of mapping explicit. These outcomes can be summarized as identifying similarities and differences as a prelude to being able to categorize. Thinking skills author Mike Lake, clarifies this: "Trying to avoid the pitfalls of over-definition and infinite reduction, I would accept (following both Feuerstein and Lipman) that the essential skills, basic to all subsequent acts of thinking and learning, are looking for differences and similarities. I use the term "looking for" rather than "seeing" to emphasize the essentially active process of successful learning."

These are the skills that underpin the ability to create maps. Maps are essentially hierarchies of categories of information, summarized using keywords in language triangles, tessellated and drawn in radiating fashion around centre and illustrated with images to facilitate memory. Every subject has its own hierarchies of information structured in ways unique to that subject.

The teacher's job is to support students in identifying relationships by comparing new information with what they already know. Three central skills – comparing, analyzing and categorizing – can be successfully taught in isolation and quickly put to use in the formulation of maps.

Maps themselves cannot be created without content. In addressing the essential nature of the material to be mapped, the skills of comparing, analyzing and categorizing are put to use. And in the process the past knowledge of the student and the characteristics of the language game (rules and distinctions) of the subject meet. It is here, at this juncture, that thinking skills become infused within the separate intellectual culture of the particular subject.

The inherent discipline of creating maps, along with the visual, concrete and explicit nature of the maps, provides a highly effective vehicle in which subject thinking can occur. Through the process of mapping, students come to understand the content. As the thinking is so visual and easy to communicate, it is open to presentation, interrogation and discourse by both teacher and student. As described in chapter 5, mapping provides a way of creating a new relationship based on partnership between the teacher and the learner.

The table on pages 73–74 details how mapping can be used to support the development of the thinking skills components described in many curriculum documents. Maps are, in fact, a direct expression of these skills. For example, chapter 5 shows how maps support students in asking relevant questions, while in chapter 6 we see how they support students in planning what to do ("Inquiry skills"). The components listed in the table under "Information processing skills" and "Creative thinking skills" – which are central to mapping – could be seen as the essential thinking skills since without these the other skills are far less likely to take place.

Mapping can no longer be seen simply as an effective means of making and taking notes, or as a technique for students with specific learning difficulties, or indeed as something for the most able. Mapping is for *all* students: it shows them how they learn and it teaches them how to learn. It does this because it makes evident, supports and develops their thinking skills. It places thinking at the heart of the curriculum because it supports the teachers' explanation and the learners' understanding.

Thinking Skills Itemized in Curriculum Documents

Thinking skills	Using mapping to develop these skills
Information processing skills These enable students to:	
• locate and collect relevant information	Mapping requires the learner to practise and develop these skills.
• sort	Information must be sorted in order to place it on the model map.
• classify	Mapping requires the learner to decide on the nature of the classification. This will depend on the purpose and context for which the map is being drawn.
• sequence	Once drawn, maps support sequencing of material since the learner is always able to see the whole and the parts at the same time.
• compare and contrast	No longer restricted by linear notes, the learner is supported in comparing and contrasting information as the map is being created. Because all elements of the problem or question can be viewed simultaneously, further comparison is possible once the map is complete.
• analyze part–whole relationships	Mapping's unique visual and organizational qualities enable the learner literally to see relationships between the parts and the whole simultaneously.
Reasoning skills These enable students to:	
• give reasons for opinions and actions	Reasons and opinions may be presented on the map. Equally, evidence to promote or support an opinion or action can be presented.
• draw inferences and make deductions	Mapping supports the learner in making informed inferences and deductions based on the principles underlying the categorization.
• use precise language	Mapping requires the learner to identify key vocabulary. The vocabulary will range from specific descriptions on the outer branches to more general and abstract terms on the central, organizing branches.
• explain what they think	Mapping offers a visual way of showing and explaining what the mapper is thinking.
• make judgments and decisions informed by reasons or evidence	The learner can use evidence and reasons made visible by mapping to make informed judgments and decisions.

Thinking skills	Using mapping to develop these skills
Inquiry Skills These enable students to:	
• ask relevant questions	Mapping when used by the teacher enables students to focus on relevant detail. When used by the learner, the process of mapping promotes relevant associations and reveals irrelevancies.
• pose and define problems	The process of mapping will make visible whatever evidence or support material the learner requires to explain her thinking.
• plan what to do and how to research	Mapping promotes thorough planning and research because it supports categorization and organizational skills. The white space on maps encourages additions and amendments.
• predict outcomes and anticipate consequences	Mapping, by making the "big picture" available to learners, makes it easier for outcomes and consequences to be considered.
• test conclusions and improve ideas	Mapping provides the learner with a way of judging his thinking against the original "big picture" and evaluating the "match". The format of the map also offers scope for easy alterations and additions.
Creative thinking skills These enable students to:	
• generate and synthesize ideas	Mapping encourages the generation and extension of ideas because the learner does not have to associate ideas in a linear fashion – it supports holographic thinking.
• suggest hypotheses	Being able to see the whole and the parts simultaneously supports the learner in suggesting hypotheses. A map is itself a hypothesis – an assertion, whose accuracy can be judged against the field of study.
• apply imagination	
• look for innovative outcomes	
Evaluation skills These enable students to:	
• evaluate information	With all aspects of information available and considered, an informed evaluation is possible.
• judge the value of what they read, hear and do·	Mapping can help learners to identify criteria for judgment and build an evidence base for informed judgments.
• develop criteria for judging the value of their own and others' work or ideas	Criteria can be mapped out and developed through discussion of the map.
• have confidence in their judgments	Judgments can be based on organized and complete models of thought.

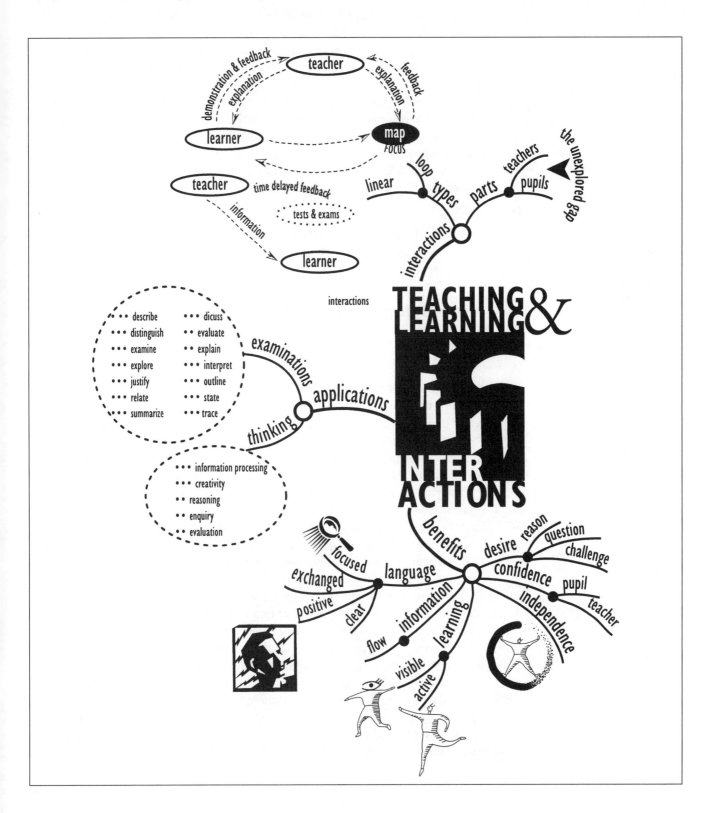

TEACHING & LEARNING & INTERACTIONS

interactions

interactions
- types
  - linear
  - loop
- parts
  - teachers
  - pupils
- map FOCUS
- the unexplored gap

teacher — demonstration & feedback / explanation → learner
teacher ← feedback / explanation ← map FOCUS
learner → map FOCUS
teacher — time delayed feedback
tests & exams
teacher — information → learner

examinations
- describe
- distinguish
- examine
- explore
- justify
- relate
- summarize
- discuss
- evaluate
- explain
- interpret
- outline
- state
- trace

thinking / applications
- information processing
- creativity
- reasoning
- enquiry
- evaluation

benefits
- language
  - focused
  - exchanged
  - positive
  - clear
- information
  - flow
- learning
  - visible
  - active
- desire
  - reason
  - question
  - challenge
- confidence
  - pupil
  - teacher
- independence

... we are used to understanding the communication between teachers and learner as the teacher teaching the learner. Seen like this, it looks like a one way, linear relationship, defined by the role. But we could look at it another way. The teacher could not teach without feedback from the learner, as the teacher only knows what to do next by the learner's response. The learner's questions, answers, and expressions, both quizzical and satisfied, let the teacher know how to proceed. So the learner elicits from the teacher exactly what they need to learn. The better the learner does this, the more skilful the teacher appears. In that sense, the learner "teaches" the teacher how to teach. And the teacher learns how to teach from the interaction. This way of understanding is different from the normal, but just as valid. Here is the origin of the saying "the best way to learn a subject is to teach it". Both teacher and learner respond to feedback in the moment and this leads to a virtuous feedback loop.

J. O'Connor and *I. McDermott*

... understanding is the product of doing, yet all too often students sit in the classroom and receive, with little being required of them other than listening, writing notes, and completing low level comprehension exercises. They receive large amounts of information but are not frequently required to do anything with it. Consequently, there is little need to think.

Mike Hughes

When someone responds to your outline of an idea or proposal by saying, "I see what you mean", are they agreeing with your proposal? Not necessarily – it's a neutral statement. Can you assume that they have successfully grasped the essence of what you have said? Not really – you do not know exactly what they have "seen".

Nevertheless, people often relate to such feedback as comforting, informative and useful. Spurred on by this apparent agreement you might carry on, embellishing the image on the canvas of the listener's mind. You might imagine that this communication is "clean" and complete, transferring faithfully the picture in your own mind directly into the imagination of your listener, like a digital transmission. Everything seems fine, until the listener's actions suggest that, despite his assertions, he hasn't actually understood a word. He definitely "saw" something, but unfortunately it probably wasn't what you were describing.

This chapter examines the nature of the exchange of knowledge in the classroom. To help you find your way around, it is divided up into the following sections:

- Identifying interactions in your classroom
- Developing a positive feedback loop using mapping
- Mapping related to task completion and examinations

Identifying interactions in your classroom

If we accept Robert Fisher's view that "we live in a mosaic of disconnected bits of experience" what can we do to help students put the mosaic together?

O'Connor and McDermott define a "system" as "an entity that maintains its existence and functions as a whole through the interaction of its parts". Using systems thinking, we could imagine ourselves helicoptering above a classroom examining the whole, the parts that make up the whole, and the connections between the parts. In order to understand how the parts are connected and work together, we must examine the whole system. The system we are going to examine here is the one in operation in your classroom.

The parts that make up the whole in your classroom are you as the teacher, your students and the environment. In this chapter, we are concerned with the human parts – you and your students. An observer looking in at your class would see you doing and hear you saying certain things. Similarly, she would see and hear your students. But what might she see going on *between* these two parts of the system in your classroom?

The quote at the beginning of the chapter describes two different systems: in the "linear" system there is a simple one-way relationship, as the teacher teaches the learner; in the other system both teacher and learner constantly respond to one another, setting up a positive feedback loop for learning. In reality, most teachers use both systems, though they may spend more time in one than in the other. However, learning is far more likely to take place in the "loop system". It may take place in the "linear" situation but if it does the teacher probably does not know for sure that it is occurring, or the *extent* to which it is occurring – until the student takes a test to find out. Mapping can support you in spending more time in the "loop system" described above.

Let us now consider which system represents a "best fit" for your current practice. Consider these questions:

1. Do you seek to establish what your students already know about a topic or area of study before teaching it?
2. Do you consider your role as being essentially one that involves delivery of the curriculum?
3. Do your students ask you questions when they do not understand?
4. Do your students get an opportunity to demonstrate what they know?
5. Do you constantly try to establish what they have or have not understood?
6. Do you know which elements of your teaching need explaining to your students?

If you have answered "no" to any of these questions (apart from question 2!), it's likely that our observer would generally perceive a one-way "linear" relationship occurring in your classroom. This is a very common, and completely understandable, situation to be in. After all, it could be said that you are the teacher so your job is to teach the curriculum. The students' job is to turn up, listen, do as they are told, and go home and try to make sense of it all.

In this "linear" system the roles are clear. Our observer can see what you the teacher and your students are doing: mostly – though not all of the time – she sees one-way traffic between you and the students. How can a teacher support a student in creating meaning and understanding if the teacher:

- does not know what her students already know about the subject
- has students who do not communicate learning needs to their teacher
- does not know what content has been understood
- does not know what language has been understood
- does not know what to explain further, or how to go about it most effectively.

The teacher cannot teach effectively without feedback from the learner. You cannot know that your explanations are working and that you are extending your student's levels of understanding and skill unless you are sure about what is going on where the learning really takes place – in the learner. Without feedback, teaching is reduced to the dissemination of information (and the management of behaviors that become part of this system) and learning is left to chance.

Developing a positive feedback loop using mapping

Mapping has enormous potential in supporting the transformation of the relationships between the learner and his own learning, and between the learner and teacher. In the past, the perceived benefits of mapping have focussed on study skills, creativity and memory applications. As important and useful as these benefits are, the opportunities that mapping can create for the learning process are even greater.

By placing and using maps at the front of the class as part of your classroom delivery, you can make your thinking (and/or the thinking of the class) visible, and therefore available, both to yourself and to the students. It is as if there is a third party in the room upon whom you and your students can focus your

Teachers have been working very hard to achieve what is both impractical and burdensome ... to cause learning in students, when of course learning must be caused by the learner ... When the goal of teaching becomes the achievement of shared meaning, a great deal of both teachers' and student's energy is released.

J. D. Novak and *D. B. Gowin*

If you believe it is your responsibility to get through to students in whatever way you have to, you will become a better teacher. However, if you claim that your responsibility is only to present information and then it's the student's responsibility to understand it, you might as well just mail them a book.

E. Jensen

A map provides people with the means to share the perceptions of others. It is a pattern made understandable.

Richard Saul Wurman

attention, rather than focusing on each other. From your own perspective, you are supported in modelling your thinking for your students.

If you are willing to show students how you have made sense of a problem, or how you have organized some information, so they will be more disposed to imitate you. You are, after all, a role model! When the thinking of the teacher or class is made "public" in this way, students who might usually find it difficult to participate in class discussions are far more likely to do so. This probably happens for several reasons. First, the map gives these students an external focus for their thoughts, which brings their attention away from any negative internal thought process ("I can't do it"). Second, the map gives students something to say; that is, the map provides key vocabulary and ideas that they can either comment on directly or use as a base for their own ideas. Third, there is already agreement in the room that what is on the board is valid or at least valued. Fourth, and most important perhaps, is the fact that your thinking has been captured, frozen, freeze-framed – unlike oral articulation. It is therefore static, "graspable" and available to your students. For many students, the use of a map will reduce their fear of failure.

Carol Hariram teaches students who have severe learning difficulties. She tells of the difference maps make to her story telling: "I had two groups on the same day. With the first group I did not have the story mapped in the background. I used props and gave a "lively" presentation of the story but at the end of the story when I asked questions none of the children could link events or any of the characters together. With the second group we mapped the story as we went along. The difference in terms of their willingness and ability to participate in discussion afterwards was amazing."

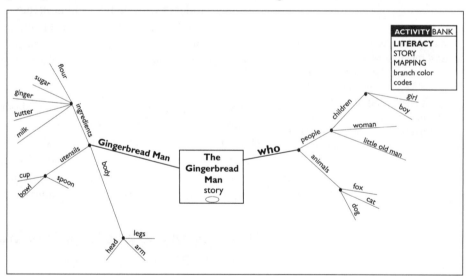

(Note that the above is a summary map for teachers. It represents the much larger, colored and "velcroed" map that was used with the students.)

With the first group there was a linear system in operation – the teacher was telling the story and the students listened. With the second group, a positive feedback cycle – a "loop system" – was in operation. The teacher had developed the children's ability to respond by creating a visual response to the story. How well does this teacher's experience mirror your own? Can you think of other possibilities for mapping stories? (See *Animal Farm* maps on pages 102 and 103.)

They [maps] stimulate active thinking, develop cognitive skills of analysis, categorization and synthesis, and provide a visual means of communication and evaluation.

Robert Fisher

When students have a map upon which to focus, they find it much easier to articulate their efforts to create meaning, and to ask questions. By asking questions the students tell you what they do not know and therefore what you need to teach (explain) next. The map supports the students in examining the learning experience being offered: they have ready access to the knowledge and ideas being presented and built upon, and they have all the information they need to weigh up arguments before coming to balanced judgments. The use of maps makes all of this easier to do and more likely to happen. Together, you and your students can examine the map, change it, add to it and weigh arguments.

Mapping promotes particular attitudes in students. By using maps students develop a desire to reason, they are more willing to challenge and they rediscover a passion to see things through to the end. As these characteristics develop, your students become more self-confident, and what Fisher terms "critical" thinkers. Such students are far more likely to participate with you in the learning process. What may once have been a linear learning relationship develops into a cyclical one; a "loop system" has been created.

When learner and teacher are successful in negotiating and sharing the meaning of a unit of knowledge, meaningful learning occurs.

Joseph Novak

In case you are not already convinced about the merits of mapping in promoting a positive feedback system, let us look closer still and consider what such a system in your classroom would "look like" to an observer. The elements described below do not exist separately from one another within the system, but it is useful to look at them separately to highlight the impact that mapping can have on the relationship between you and your students.

Conversation

Perhaps the most obvious difference our observer might notice is that a positive exchange of language is occurring in the classroom between you and your students – a conversation.

As any photographer knows, the frame of the viewfinder "organizes" the image within it, creating a visual statement where, without the frame, one might get only clutter.

D.N. Perkins

In a linear relationship the teacher does most of the talking and the student is a passive recipient of this language. You may well be very good at explaining what you are teaching, but how do you know that your students are understanding what you say? With a map present, the students can see the structure within which your words should make sense. They also have a structure to help them question what you are saying. They can be specific about what they have or have not understood. They can teach you how to teach them.

Because they no longer have to interpret what you are saying, your students are freed up to listen to what you are saying. In addition, they are able to use the model that they have examined, questioned and developed with their own ideas as a structure to support their writing.

Flow of information

Mapping can help information flow to, from and among students and teachers ... Most importantly children learn a procedure for investigating, visualizing and organizing information.

Robert Fisher

The second interaction that our observer might see is a flow of information between yourself and the students – not a one-day "dissemination" followed by a delay as they write an essay, complete an exercise or do a test, but an ongoing collaboration of teacher and students.

Rather than supporting a passive teaching/learning environment, mapping encourages children to be actively engaged in thinking, to elaborate and build on ideas.

Robert Fisher

If teachers want their young students to have robust dispositions to investigate, hypothesize, experiment, and so forth, they might consider making their own such intellectual dispositions more visible to their children.

L.G. Katz

The sole task of an education system should be to give you the tools and provide you with a critical mind, so that you can ask the right questions, make the right connections.

Richard Saul Wurman

In addition to an increase in production, I have found that mapping encourages students to think in more concrete terms about the concepts behind what they are learning. Model mapping encourages clearer thinking and I have seen a commensurate growth in student confidence because they are more sure of their reasoning. Mapping takes students through each stage of the thinking process and puts an order to it. Instead of following 'will-o-the-wisp' trains of thought and arriving at a conclusion, students can now identify the steps which will lead them there, and most importantly can replicate the process.

Val Hill, Teacher

Active learning

Most importantly, perhaps, mapping provides you with another means of ensuring that active learning takes place in your classroom – not formal, direct instruction and not undirected meaningless "copy-and-color" activity, but active learning. When active learning takes place, students engage their natural capacities to be interested, curious and co-operative, to enquire and to analyze. We cannot force students to engage in learning, nor should we try to. We can, however provide a system in which they can usefully engage.

Using mapping related to task completion and examinations

Mapping can be used to help students develop some of the key skills they will need as they study in school and tackle examinations.

The table on page 81 lists some reasoning skills using terms that are commonly found in classroom tasks and examination papers. Mapping can be used by the teacher to illustrate and explain what is meant by this "examination vocabulary" as it is a visible expression of the skill being developed. It supports the student in carrying out the skill described (see table).

So, mapping can support your students in developing their reasoning skills. This is important for learning, because they reason (or work things out) in order to create personal meaning or understanding for themselves.

Task examination wording	How mapping supports the student in carrying out each skill
• **Describe** ... give a detailed account	The learner has access to detail and structures underlying the detail on a map.
• **Discuss** ... investigate or examine by argument	The learner has a clear structure to support discussion and the map supports the addition or inclusion of new arguments and ideas.
• **Distinguish between** ... indicate the difference between	The learner can see and therefore point to the differences.
• **Evaluate** ... give your judgments about the merits of theories or opinions	With all features present the learner can make supported judgments.
• **Examine** ... look closely into	The learner can analyze all the details.
• **Explain** ... make plain, interpret and account for; give reasons for	The learner can illustrate her thinking.
• **Explore** ... examine thoroughly, consider from a variety of viewpoints	The learner can examine thoroughly and can add ideas at will.
• **Interpret** ... make clear and explicit; show the meaning of	The very structure of the map demonstrates the interpretation. The structure reminds the learner of her thinking.
• **Justify** ... show adequate grounds for decisions and conclusions	The learner has all the supporting information readily available at the same time.
• **Outline** ... give the main features or general principles of a subject omitting minor details and emphasizing structure and interactions	The learner can see the essential elements and mapping provides the structure.
• **Relate** ... show how things are connected to each other, and to what extent they are alike or affect each other	The learner can see existing relationships between concepts and can create new ones.
• **State** ... present in a brief, clear form	Essential language and concepts are evident.
• **Summarize** ... give a concise account of the chief points of a matter, omitting details and examples	Central branches hold the main ideas.
• **Trace** ... follow the development or history of a topic from some point of origin	The learner can "polebridge" her understanding.

6 Maps in the classroom

practical examples through a unit of work

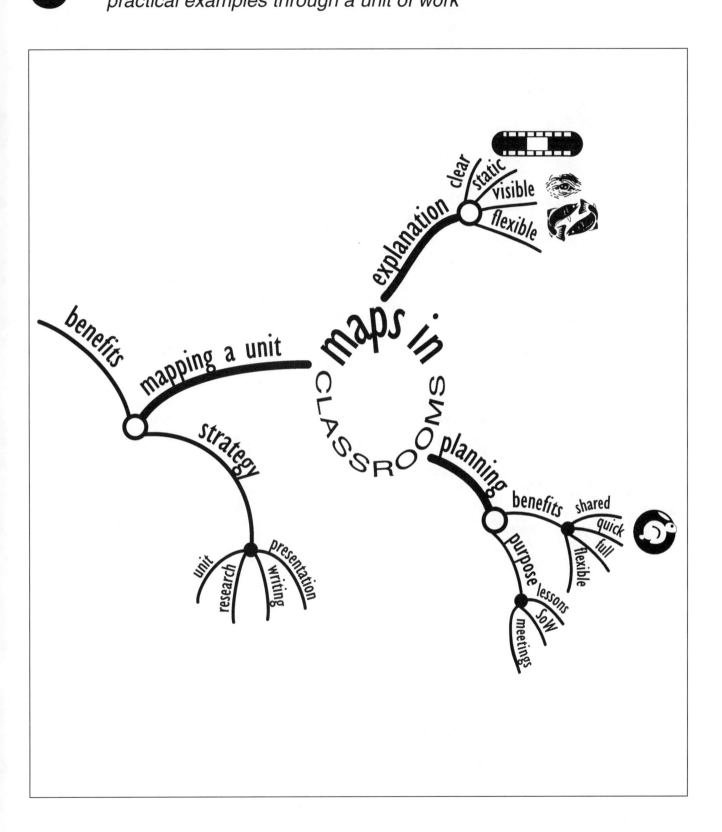

An old joke, no doubt, but how many times have you felt it would be better to start from a different place when you were lost in a sea of information? It is easy to feel overwhelmed and anxious if you cannot establish reference points when working through new material. You need a perspective that will show you the "big picture".

When you can see a big picture, reference points are secured and you can make out options for traversing the terrain. A previously confusing mass of information becomes conquerable as its parts are integrated into the big picture through connections to other locations on the map. You begin to make meaning out of previously disconnected perspectives. Understanding emerges.

This chapter is divided up into the following sections:

- Explanation
- Planning
- Mapping throughout a unit of work

Explanation

The core purpose of education is to support learners in creating meaning and understanding for themselves. Everything we do as educators should forward this aim. One of our primary tools for this is explanation.

A dictionary might define the term "explain" as "to make plain or clear, to show the meaning of "; this is exactly what a map does.

Effective explanation in the classroom is actually a two-way process. By using maps you can reveal to your students your understanding about the topic or concepts of the lesson. They can literally *see* what you are saying. By the same token, you can see what they have understood from their own maps.

Maps can give a massive boost to teacher confidence. By drawing a map you are forced to examine your own understanding and to clarify your explanation. Once the map is done, you need never be unsure about how the content fits together nor need you have any concerns about the students being able to "see" what you mean.

The message is simple: using maps is an effective way of supporting clear teacher explanation and student understanding.

You cannot start to explain anything to students until you know what they already know. Explanation can only take place when new information is based on and linked to the learner's existing knowledge. If you do not know what they know, you are left making a lot of assumptions about your teaching and their learning.

The importance of finding out what students know is illustrated by the work of Wragg and Brown. They describe how a student teacher introduced volcanoes to two different groups. With the first group she did not spend any time finding out what they already knew. She introduced the topic by saying, "Today I want to tell you a little bit about volcanoes. Here is a model of one and you can see that this is the crater and, as you probably know, this is the lava, and this part here is called the magma chamber. Perhaps you have heard of volcanoes before. There is one in Italy called Vesuvius ..."

With the second group the teacher showed the children the model and asked if anyone knew anything about volcanoes. You will not be surprised to hear that a mass of information came from the group that surpassed what she herself had told the first group. The second group, for example, knew the names of several volcanoes and their locations; they knew that volcanic dust could travel thousands of miles in air streams; they knew about Icelandic geysers and terms like "lava" and "eruption".

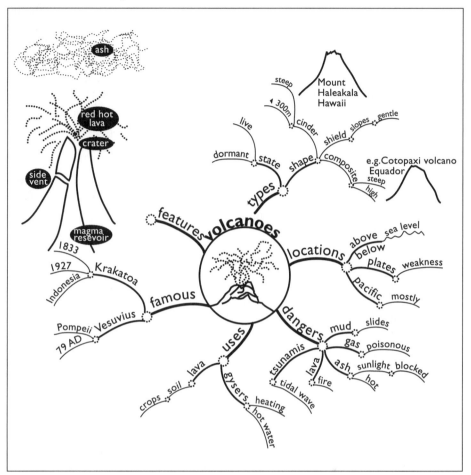

With the second group, the teacher was able to establish what they knew and identify the level of language that the group was happy with. She was able to identify any misconceptions that the students had about volcanoes.

A map can be used to capture the current mental model held by an individual or a group about a particular topic. The work of the teacher above with the second group of students was obviously useful. If she had drawn a model map of their understanding, not only would she and the students have been able to see clearly what they collectively knew, they would also have been able to see exactly how the students' understanding was developing as the topic progressed.

Using model maps produced by a whole class or group is a very powerful teaching and learning tool. You could use the DOM or the Think-Pair-Share method for doing this. DOM stands for "Dump, Organize and Map", and involves a class discussion about the topic followed by a random "dumping" of the information generated on one section of the board. This information is then organized (grouped) before being mapped.

Think-Pair-Share is carried out in exactly the same way as DOM, except that the information to be mapped is generated by the students in a slightly different way. First ask the students to think of one, three or five words to do with the topic, before asking them to pair up and compare. Each pair then shares their information with another pair, and then the group of four teams up with another

The children do their concept map at the beginning of a unit of work or topic; for example, year 4 did a concept map at the beginning of a science topic on solids and liquids. The children did this as a whole class map initially, and then, once modelled, attempted to do individual maps.

Mrs. Chowdhury, Teacher

group before the students feedback to you. You then "dump" the class' information on the board, organize it and map it – all the time discussing with the students how to go about this. In this way, you and the students make sense of the information together, as you create meaning and therefore understanding.

Now that you know what your students know, you can build on this. Explanation is supported because you are providing students with a picture of their growing understanding. If a point is reached where the students do not understand, they are able to use the map to help them explain to you exactly what they do not understand. Because she can see the whole picture and the individual components of the whole at the same time, the learner is better aware of the significance of what she has not understood. The teacher and learner can see this simultaneously.

As you read through the rest of this chapter, keep this key theme of "explanation" at the forefront of your thinking. In particular, look at how this notion of understanding is cemented in the sub-section on mapping through a unit of work (page 89).

Planning

This section is divided up under the following headings:

- Making your thinking public
- Planning for teachers
- Planning for students

Making your thinking public

Consider this – as a teacher you aim to give students the product or outcome of your thinking, but do you give away the thinking itself? You have undoubtedly, over the years, got better at selecting and organizing the information and methods for your lessons. You also have a strong grip on your subject area generally, its language, structure and the thinking required to create meaning and understanding. You could say that you have become confident and knowledgable in the pedagogy of your subject. How can you communicate this confidence and knowledge to your students?

Teachers successfully give students the benefit or product of their thinking and understanding, but rarely share with the students how they themselves have understood the topic; they often expect students to understand without explaining how they made sense of the content in the first place. This, in effect, is asking the students to work it out for themselves, from scratch – to do a jigsaw puzzle without the box lid. When you use mapping to set out a scheme of work, a topic overview or a lesson plan, you create a model of your thinking, which is then public and open to examination.

There are, however, two pitfalls in physically demonstrating to your students how you have understood and organized the subject information. First, you must stress that this is only your interpretation of how the information goes together. Always be open to alternatives and invite students to suggest other possible models. The usefulness of the mapping technique lies in the process and not necessarily in the result. Maps are only models of reality and are therefore only interpretations. This will become obvious when you see the range of different models, or interpretations, of a topic that students produce when they plan projects, essays or presentations using maps.

Second, your map may well not make total sense to your students (or to anyone else for that matter) until you "think aloud" your mapping process. In order for students to understand your thinking you need to take them through it – "walk" them through it – explaining your understanding of it as you go.

Planning for teachers

The upper map on the next page shows a social studies teacher's overview of a unit of work covering the origins of World War II. Notice that the Italian invasion of Ethiopia takes up only a few centimetres of space. The lower map shows how the teacher then expanded on the Ethiopian Crisis by drawing a whole map on it as a single lesson plan.

The content of a map depends on the context and purpose for which you are creating it. You can map a year's work, a unit of work, or an individual lesson. Once created, the map is a physical representation – a model – of your thoughts. It can be amended in any way you see fit. There is room for additions. You may even see areas that you want to omit.

On a map, you can simultaneously see the whole picture and the pieces that make up the whole. No longer dependent on memory to keep disparate parts of the topic together in your mind's eye, you are better able to see relationships between the pieces and the whole. You can highlight relationships on the map by using keys, arrows and color. Similarly, because you don't need to turn pages to remind yourself of the full story, you are supported in seeing how best to sequence, resource and deliver each scheme, unit or lesson.

Your planning map can probably be used to meet school or district planning requirements that you may have to complete. It can also be used with students to provide an overview of work to be covered and to help reveal the prior learning that they bring to the subject, to which new learning can be connected.

Below, a teacher describes her experience of working with a colleague who used mapping as a planning tool.

> "Before, I would plod along using the school's existing forms of 'boxed' planning – a non-creative form which, to my mind, didn't seem to allow for any imagination or free thinking.

> "At first, I found planning with [my colleague] a nightmare. I found pinning her down was fairly impossible as mentioning the 'P' word would throw up a 'rigid system' wall in her brain; it seemed to block her creativity. I used to read categories from the planning sheet to her, but she seemed stifled by the structure.

> "After a while, she would wander around the classroom, not looking at the planning sheet, but simply talking about one idea, then another. I'd be sitting, trying to fit her ideas into the boxes, until she'd start to write keywords on the whiteboard, hitting on one amazing idea after another, and I'd have to screw up the paper and start again. Then I realized that if I went along with her and memory mapped the ideas, later I could fit them into the boxes."

Mapping strategies can allow teachers to cover topics in greater depth.
Robert Fisher

What matters most is the modelling process and not the model.
Ian Harris

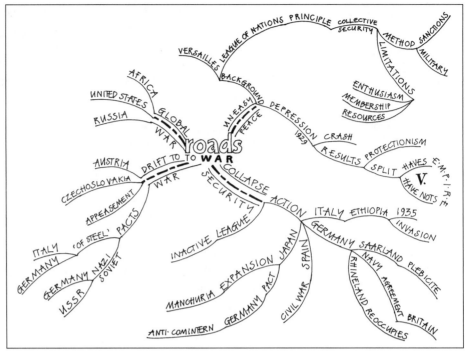

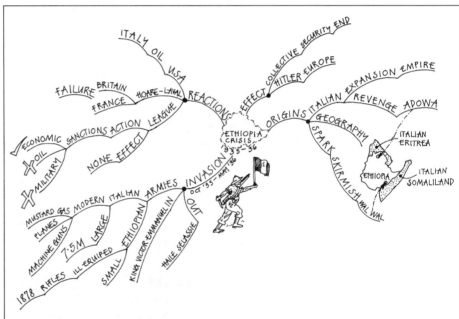

Planning for students

When told that 20% of the marks for Business Studies went on planning, a student at Chigwell High School in Essex pointed out politely to the teacher that "nobody has ever taught us how to plan!"

The authors spent three hours with the group, and taught them how to map. For homework, their teacher asked the students to plan a presentation for the following week based on units of work that they had covered during the year so far. A week later, their human resources maps had been reduced onto overhead transparencies and the students presented their maps to their peers. One of their maps is shown on the next page.

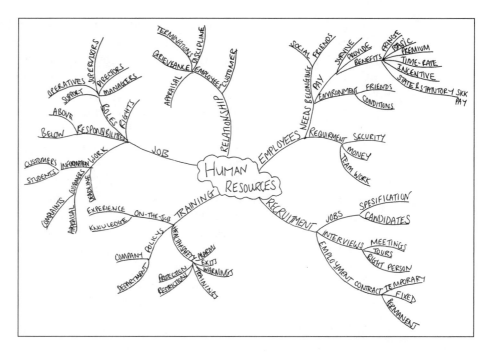

Students can use mapping to plan any aspect of their work at school and at home. Students who use mapping as a planning tool can expect to find their planning easier and more effective; they can expect to be better able to manage their homework and revision; they can expect to be able to demonstrate and communicate their understanding more readily. At the end of the day, they can expect better examination results.

Mapping through a unit of work

If you use a map to help you complete a journey not only does it confirm that you have arrived at your intended destination, it also shows you where you are on the way.

The ability to express an idea is well nigh as important as the idea itself.

Bernard Barush, US Statesman

If you, as the teacher, provide students with map overviews of the units and individual elements of their study, they can see where they are and where they are going. By asking students to produce their own map at various stages of a unit of work, you can see how much they have added to their understanding. The same map can usually be used at each stage because students are adding new key information to existing levels of understanding. Give out a sheet of paper at the beginning of a topic and ask pupils to build a picture of their understanding as they go through the work. In this way, you are measuring progress; they are demonstrating their learning.

There is a tendency for teachers to view mapping simply as a good tool for revision and planning. But maps are perhaps most powerful when used by the learner to explain or demonstrate her learning. The process of producing a map is at least as valuable as the product itself.

A psychology teacher describes her experience of mapping: "I used a mapping photocopy master pack and subject-specific content to teach my students how to map. As it turned out, this provided a useful revision exercise – it was not time away from our work at all in the end. After the initial instruction, I had a much clearer idea about the levels my students were working at. I then put the students into groups of three or four and asked them to collaboratively produce a map relating to a particular area of their study that I gave each group. After a brief period (my students were not comfortable or familiar with working collaboratively on such a focused task in this way), I watched amazed as they engaged in very deep dialogue about the work we had covered in psychology. A colleague popped in and stayed ... equally amazed. We were witnessing students discussing how they were shaping and organizing their thinking. By model mapping, they were producing a model of their understanding ... I can see what is missing in terms of my explanation, planning and delivery."

At the conclusion of a unit of work, you may wish to have students demonstrate their understanding by producing a map of a book or work studied. Ask students to prepare a map to summarize the unit or to organize their thoughts about selected topics in the unit – perhaps related to a writing assignment or a formal presentation. (See Animal Farm maps on pages 102 and 103 and Earth in Space on page 108.)

Mapping is particularly valuable when students complete a research project, probably at the conclusion of a unit of study. The following strategy for completing research is enhanced through mapping.

1. Students select or review their research topic and discuss the purpose, audience and presentational format (e.g., essay, formal talk, audiovisual presentation) for the research.
2. Students identify key questions related to their topic. Often three or four key questions are adequate.
3. Students identify sources to answer their questions – class notes including maps; print resources including textbooks; interviews; Internet.
4. Once the questions have been established, students employ sources to answer each question and organize information gathered under each question.
5. Students employ their notes to complete a draft.
6. Students revise their draft.
7. Students present their research to an audience.

Students who are familiar with mapping can list their topics (and possibly purpose, audience and format) at the centre of the map. The key questions become the main branches for the map. Information gathered can be organized under sub-headings. Students quickly realize when further information is required because sub-headings lack detail. The map becomes an excellent pre-writing tool and a useful guide as students complete their drafts. (See Nutrition map on page 100.)

Cleverness and internal maps

understanding how we understand

This chapter is divided up into the following sections:

- Distinguishing cleverness
- Giving it away
- Putting cleverness into schools

Distinguishing cleverness

Can you remember individuals from your own school days who won all the academic awards? We admire their results and are left feeling that they have something special we just don't have – they seem to have some sort of secret that they won't share. The very features of their cleverness are probably not well known to them. They are unaware of what it is that distinguishes them from their fellow human beings. Clearly, they are aware of the effect their thinking has on others – admiration, validation, perhaps envy. What is not apparent is how the product (story, report, essay, exam result) was achieved. In other words, how did the "cleverness" work? They know that they are clever but do not know how they are clever.

We do not see what clever people do, only the final result. Simply getting to see the final product of clever thinking certainly impresses with its brilliance, but it is not empowering. What if we could make intelligence public and have it in front of us, so we could have a good look at it? What would we see that clever people actually do? Let us try to demystify cleverness and to democratize it – to "give it away".

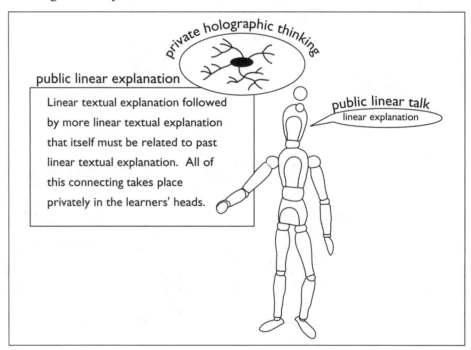

Even a clever person might not find it easy to explain how his cleverness works. There seems to be no ready model available that makes the invisible visible, the abstract concrete, the ephemeral permanent, the fleeting static or the private public. But this is exactly what we need to do in order to "capture" the private nature of cleverness.

Every map takes the limits of his own field of vision for the limits of the world.

Arthur Schopenhaur, nineteenth century philosopher

Neuroscience has discovered a great deal about neurons and synapses, but not nearly enough to guide educational practice. Currently, the span between brain and learning cannot support much of a load. Too many people marching in step across it could be dangerous. If we are looking for a basic science to help guide educational practice and policy, cognitive psychology is a much better bet.

J. T. Bruer

Mental models are the images, assumptions, and stories which we carry in our minds of ourselves, other people, institutions, and every aspect of the world. Like a pane of glass framing and subtly distorting our vision, mental models determine what we see.

P. Senge

The only real voyage of discovery consists not in seeking new landscapes but in having new eyes.

Marcel Proust

We are all natural model builders.

P. Senge

Man looks at his world through transparent patterns or templates which he creates and then attempts to fit over the realities of which the world is composed. The fit is not always very good. Yet without such patterns the world appears to be such an undifferentiated homogeneity that man is unable to make any sense out of it. Even a poor fit is more helpful to him than nothing at all.

George A. Kelly

There have been many ways of looking at intelligence. These perspectives shape our view of intelligence and offer some insights into the working of cleverness itself. On the whole, these perspectives, or models, tell us how cleverness manifests itself in actions, attitudes, attributes and strategies. Howard Gardner's multiple intelligences model, for example, sets out eight areas of intelligence that we can identify in students in school. This is a useful model. It supports us in providing a greater variety of experiences for students, and shows where we are perhaps being too narrow in our approach. However, it does not tell us what happens when this intelligence is working – it doesn't explain "how they did it".

Models of intelligence do not, therefore, offer any great lever into knowing how clever people are clever. For that we need another distinction.

We know that we receive information through our senses. But how exactly do we transform our sense impressions into coherent views of the world? What mechanisms are there that allow for the meaningful absorption of new information? How do we know what we know?

This is where cognitive psychologists tell us more than neuroscientists. The last ten years have produced 95% of our understanding of how the brain learns and this better understanding has led teachers to be more skilful in promoting positive states for learning. It has not, however, added to our understanding of how our minds are constructed.

By "mind", we mean the fabric of meaning developed in each individual that constitutes a world view; a consciousness even. We could say that our minds are the shape, or collection of shapes, arrived at by making sense of our experiences. As Professor Susan Greenfield puts it, "... throughout life the brain will be in constant dialogue with the environment as one interprets and reinforces experiences in the light of what has gone before. It is this personalization of the brain that is inextricable from memories, that for me is the best biological definition of a 'mind'."

The technical term for this sense of shape is "schema". Schema is a term well known to students of psychology, while in the business world people refer to "mental models". The use of these terms is normally restricted to these domains.

Mental models or schemas are central factors in understanding, thinking and learning – factors that affect all of us, all our lives. When you try to solve a practical problem, a personal difficulty or a logistical crisis in your mind, by the end of the thought process you have worked out a way of understanding it; of gathering, collecting and organizing your thoughts so that the problem makes sense. The organization of your thinking is a schema. Even if you can't make sense of the problem, the thought that says "I can't make sense of it" is a schema too.

Daniel Goleman describes schemas as "The packets that organize information and make sense of experience". They "embody the rules and categories that order raw experience into coherent meaning".

If you think about it long enough, it becomes apparent that all knowledge and experience is packaged in schemas. "Schemas are the ghost in the machine, the intelligence that guides information as it flows through the mind." Humans go on creating schemas all their lives, to deal with minute details and vast domains, from concrete bodily experiences to abstract feelings. As Rumelhart, a cognitive psychologist, explains schemas capture and organize everything: "Schemas can represent knowledge at all levels – from ideologies and cultural truths to knowledge about what constitutes an appropriate sentence in our language to knowledge about the meaning of a particular word to knowledge about what patterns of [sounds] are associated with what letters of the alphabet".

Once we have captured our interpretations of our experiences in schemas, we can refer to them, compare them and organize them. In this way, we can reason about them. This is why schemas are the key to bringing the private nature of cleverness into a public forum.

We know from recent research into schemas that they have "shape" and that they capture the essence of concepts, events and experience. But how are schemas created? The way this happens is described by cognitive psychologist, Marshall, who tells us that: "A schema is a vehicle of memory, allowing organization of an individual's similar experiences in such a way that the individual:

1. can easily recognize additional experiences that are also similar, discriminating between these and ones that are dissimilar
2. can access a generic framework that contains the essential elements of all these similar experiences, including verbal and non-verbal components
3. can draw inferences, make estimates, create goals and develop plans using the framework, and
4. can utilize skills, procedures or rules as needed when faced with a problem for which this particular framework is relevant".

Put simply, the creation of schemas takes place through organization. The world and the individual interact perpetually. The interactions are in themselves meaningless; things just happen, and the individual adds meaning to them. The meaning resides in the meaning-maker, not in the event.

As Ian's story illustrates, it is through the creation of schemas that we create our experience of our lives.

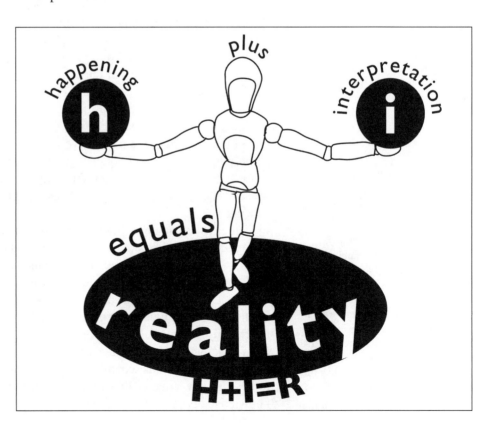

It is in human nature to create meaning from experience, and indeed it is probably essential for independent survival. We create meaning by organizing the "labels" that we attach to our experiences. It has been shown that infants of 3 and 4 months can organize and conceptualize their experiences, even though they don't yet have language skills, and even though almost every experience in their young lives is a new one. So, we start very early, and continue to organize the meanings into ever more complex structures throughout our lives. These collections of meanings themselves create higher order meanings. This grasping for meaning is not passive but active – it is the way we understand.

Structures of meaning are built through hierarchical organization, as shown in the illustration below. This is a traditional way of representing classification graphically. Goleman does not suggest that we consciously construct these diagrams in visual format in our heads. The diagram is not supposed to be a direct representation of thinking. It is a model or analogy of thinking.

So, all our thinking is structured along the same hierarchical lines as those used to describe schemas. We create categories of information, organized into hierarchies, and forge novel links between them based on each new experience.

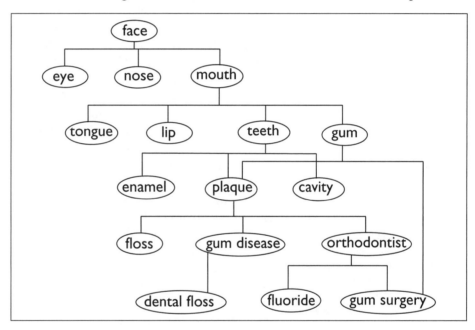

Clever people do exactly the same, but in more elaborate ways, making many more links and cross-connections between schemas. This allows them to:

- assimilate a great deal of information
- see connections between categories, and identify characteristics that either include or exclude items from categories
- switch focus quickly from overarching concept to peripheral detail
- recognize positions along the hierarchy of categories
- refashion the principles of the categorization in order, to create a different arrangement or "big picture"
- create new ideas and possibilities by seeing original relationships between categories
- store this architecture in a retrievable form.

The mind, we are convinced, selectively builds purposive models – paradigms – of events, using these to govern and increase its purchase on experience.

G. A. Woditsch

[An expert's] artistry is evident in his selective management of large amounts of information.

Donald Schon

Cognitive mapping is one way that we can try to make visible a conceptual structure, not simply to see what it is, but to process it, to challenge it and help enlarge it.

Robert Fisher

This theory is supported by studies looking at the complexities of people's maps of ideas and understanding. Marshall has found that "the more connections an individual makes at this level, the greater the understanding on the part of that individual". Novak has recognized, in relation to concept mapping, that the more cross-connections are made the better the grasp on the subject. These cross-connections are not always obvious, and require a great deal of creativity to see them. They depend on the basic structure being in place in order to see beyond and across the fundamental organization of content.

When used as models, visual maps – because their structure is dependent on the same hierarchical organization of information upon which our thinking is based – offer a very powerful means of making private thinking public; of turning rapid decisions into static trails; of transforming abstractions to graspable graphics. Maps represent thinking in a visible way. They are the vehicle for sharing cleverness.

Giving it away

There are now many attempts to capture and share others' intelligence or "cleverness". In a review of studies of novices learning from experts, Marshall explains the attempts to catch private thinking: "For the most part, this new methodology [concept mapping] shifts attention away from the end product of reasoning and focuses instead on early and intermediate steps, which are usually unobservable. To tap into these unobserved processes, researchers ask their subjects to describe in detail their mental reasoning as they solve problems."

Academics have spent decades studying how professionals pass on their expertise. However, asking people to commentate on their thinking processes while they are taking place is problematic. Research into this area has found that subjects were considerably hampered by this demand: "Verbalization may cause such a ruckus in the front of one's mind that one is unable to attend to the new approaches that may be emerging in the back of one's mind".

This problem is acknowledged by management guru Paul Miller. Perhaps without realizing quite how close he was to finding the way to achieve an answer to the problem, he notices that: "Soft knowledge ... is difficult and at times impossible to access ... You need a map to get to any destination – unless you have been to the place before. The information can come directly from the map, from someone else who has a map, or someone who has it 'in their head'".

A map of course makes this thinking public, static, graspable. These three qualities make one further benefit possible – shared explanation.

Putting cleverness into schools

Perhaps, then, what we mean by "being clever" is no more than the combination of the apparently opposite skills of organization and creativity. We can see that they are totally dependent on each other. Novel connections cannot be made until the basic structure is laid down. The organization of content allows for this creative perspective. Without the content being hierarchically classified, there would be no patterns to discern. In education, we have adopted the notion of left- and right-brain functions enthusiastically. The neuroscientists who make these discoveries are frustrated by the misleading popularization of their discoveries and their inappropriate adoption by educators.

The lists of hemispheric faculties do often obscure more basic distinctions. Particular skills may indeed have particular locations in the brain, but we need to ask ourselves whether this information has any real significance. In other words, is this information merely interesting rather than empowering? Surely it is more useful to be able to recognize the relationships between creativity and organization and between wholeness and parts.

The use of maps encourages the use of both organizational and creative faculties. Maps demand the user to organize and they tease the user to be creative. They demonstrate the thinking behind the product; the "ghost in the machine" is revealed. Cleverness is demystified and made evident. A model of what was internal – "in the head" – has come out into the open. The abstract and private nature of schemas is transformed, through model maps, into the concrete and public. Blinding speed of thought has been captured in time, freeze-framed – a whole perspective has been captured and pictured. Now, we have the means of modelling cleverness.

If you wanted to learn a new activity such as golf, you might watch golf on the television, and soon after you might buy a book about golf techniques. This would start you using the language of golf. About the same time, you would probably start to buy a few golf clubs and try them out. Your participation at a golf club would give you contact with other golfers, both novices and expert. From both you would receive feedback on your technique. At this time, you might also pay for lessons. All these activities would, in their different ways, provide instruction on developing your golfing skills. The instruction would be related to the visible actions that constitute golfing – people are able to see what you're doing, and feed back accordingly.

If you were to learn any other skill, the same sort of learning process could take place, but with thinking, learning and understanding there is no obvious parallel. With the pervasive use of maps, however, we can move closer to the golfing analogy in which the learner can benefit from continual and instant feedback from those around her.

If a whole school were to adopt mapping, it might be possible to duplicate the culture of obvious and natural learning that takes place outside of school. Students could watch their expert peers "doing" thinking, "thinking aloud" through their maps. School policies, student materials and posters could demonstrate constantly the mechanics of mapping, as well as the principles of the subject content. Different subjects would offer different terrains in which to practice mapping skills. Teachers and students could be coaches for personal instruction. "Star mappers" could hold clinics to demonstrate and explain their strategies; master classes could develop additional refinements. Talk among students and staff would be explicit, making direct references to the public, shared maps. Feedback would be ongoing assessment for learning rather than stressful assessment of learning. Cleverness would be a graspable, shared commodity, out in the open and available to all.

Gallery of maps

This section includes a wide range of maps that were created by students, teachers and the authors of this book. These maps can be used in the classroom in a variety of ways. You many choose to:

- Refer to the maps as they are mentioned in the text to consolidate your learning, for example, (See Nutrition map on page 100).
- Photocopy the maps and post them in your classroom to serve as examples and models for yourself and students.
- Introduce the concept of mapping to students by walking them through one of the maps in the Gallery of Maps. Good examples are Nutrition (page 100), First Aid (page 101) or Mapping: Methodology and Application (page 113).
- Use the maps to inspire your own ideas for mapping.

Below are the maps included in this section.

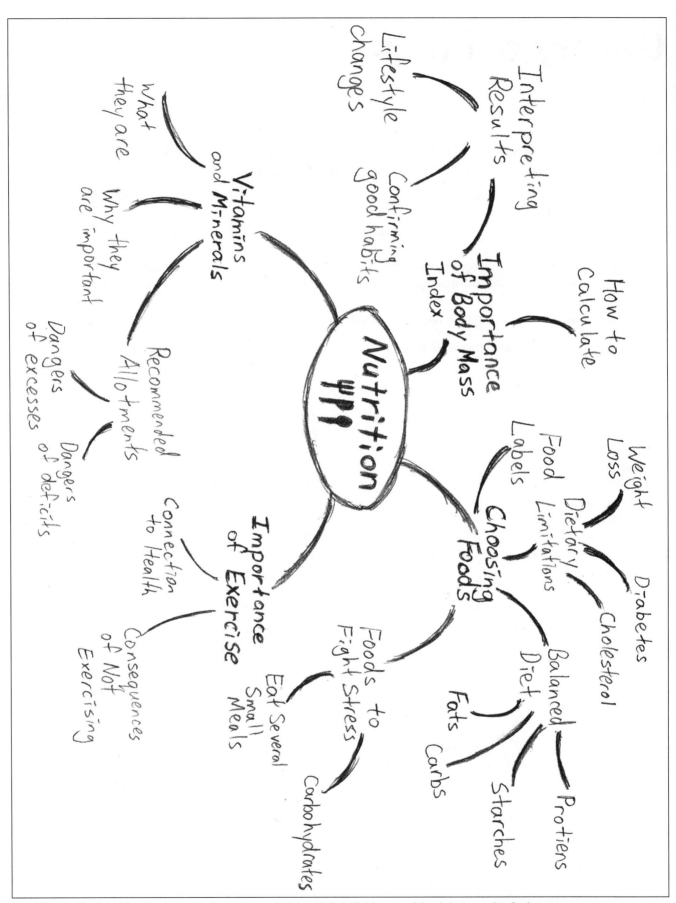

Nutrition

Importance of Body Mass Index
- Interpreting Results
  - Lifestyle changes
  - Confirming good habits
- How to Calculate

Choosing Foods
- Food Labels
  - Weight Loss
  - Diabetes
  - Cholesterol
- Dietary Limitations
- Balanced Diet
  - Fats
  - Carbs
    - Starches
    - Proteins
- Foods to Fight Stress
  - Eat Several Small Meals
  - Carbohydrates

Importance of Exercise
- Connection to Health
- Consequences of Not Exercising

Vitamins and Minerals
- What they are
- Why they are important
- Recommended Allotments
  - Dangers of excesses
  - Dangers of deficits

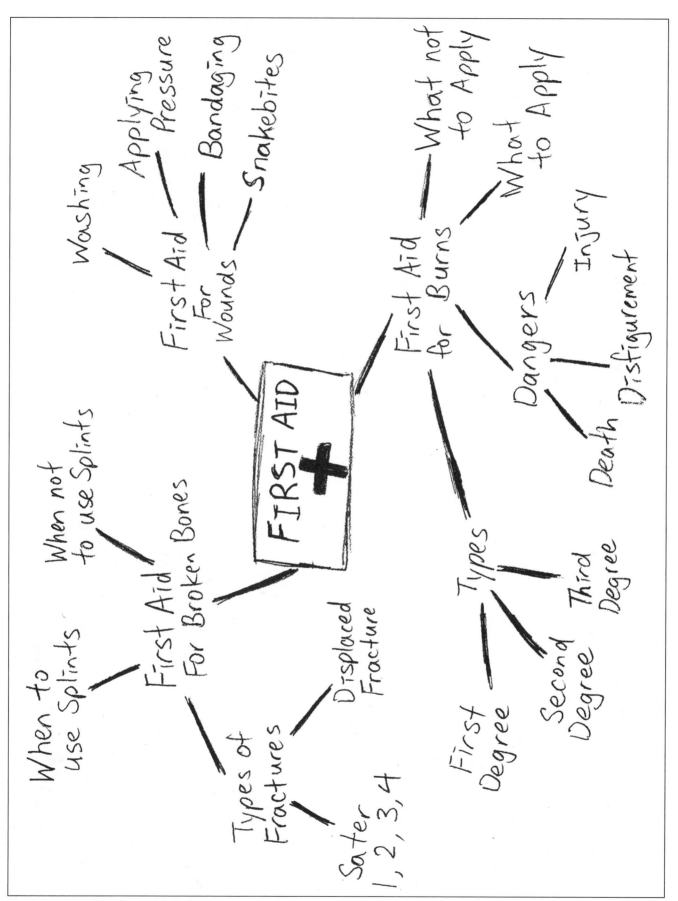

FIRST AID

Washing
Applying Pressure
Bandaging
Snakebites
First Aid For Wounds

What not to Apply
What to Apply
First Aid for Burns
Dangers
Injury
Death
Disfigurement

When to use Splints
When not to use Splints
First Aid For Broken Bones
Types of Fractures
Displaced Fracture
Sater 1, 2, 3, 4

Types
First Degree
Second Degree
Third Degree

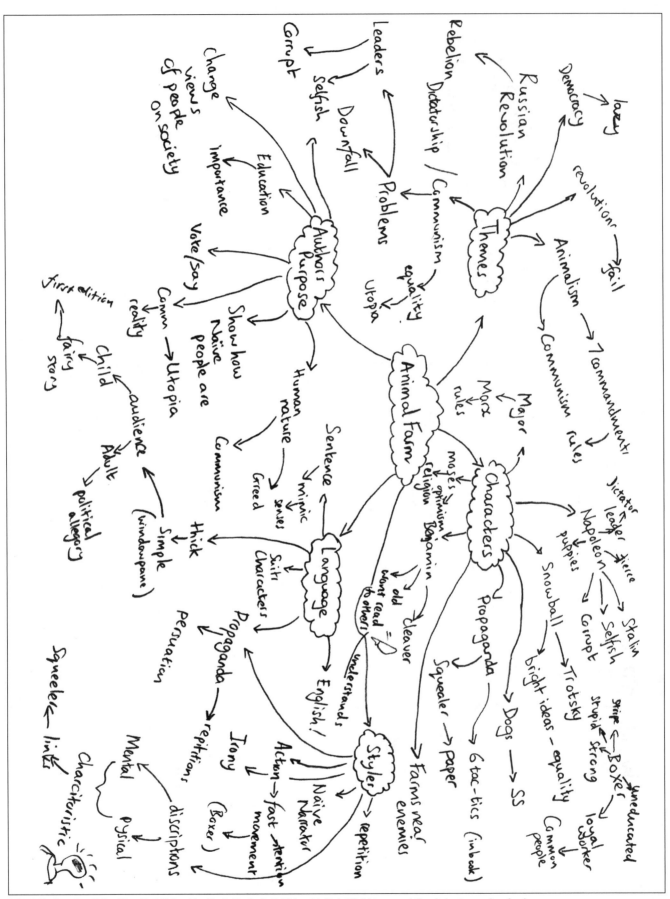

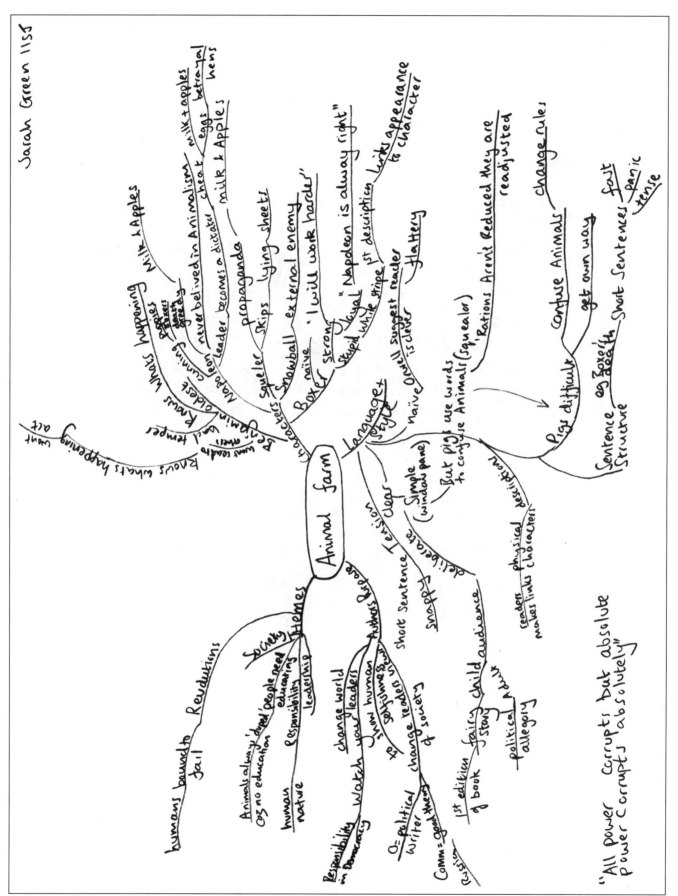

Sarah Green 11SS

Animal Farm

Happening
- Milk & Apples
- apples
- sheep dying
- starving wheels happening

Characters
- Benjamin oldest
- Napoleon cunning
- bad temper
- knows what's happening
- others ready to
- Knows what's happening won't tell

- never believed in Animalism — milk + apples
- leader becomes a dictator
- cheat eggs betrayal hens
- milk & APPLES

Propaganda
- Squealer skips / lying sheets

- Snowball naive external enemy
- Boxer strong "I will work harder"
- stupid white stripe
- "Napoleon is always right"
- naive
- 1st description
- Links appearance to character

Language + Style
- Flattery
- suggest reader is clever
- naive Orwell
- But pigs use words to confuse Animals (squealer)
- 'Rations Aren't Reduced they are readjusted'
- change rules
- Confuse Animals
- Pigs difficult get own way
- Sentence as Orwells death Short Sentences fast panic tense
- Sentence Structure

Tension
- deliberate clear
- Single (window pane)
- Short Sentence
- snappy
- readers physical description makes links characters

Themes
- humans bound to fail
- Revolutions
- Society
- Animals always duped
- 'dumb' people need educating
- cos no education
- Responsibility
- leadership
- human nature
- change world
- Watch your leaders
- how human authors Purpose
- to get human readers to change readers of society
- Q= political writer
- Comm = good theme
- revision
- 1st edition fairy story child audience book
- political allegory

"All power Corrupts But absolute Power Corrupts absolutely"

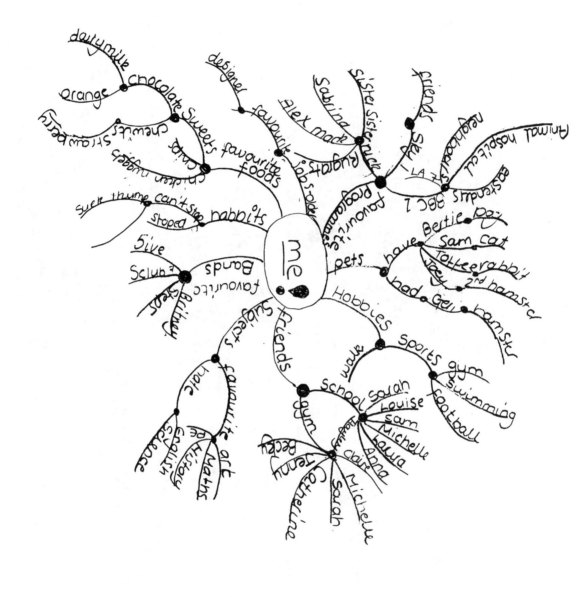

Charlotte
Howarth.

Laura Wenborn

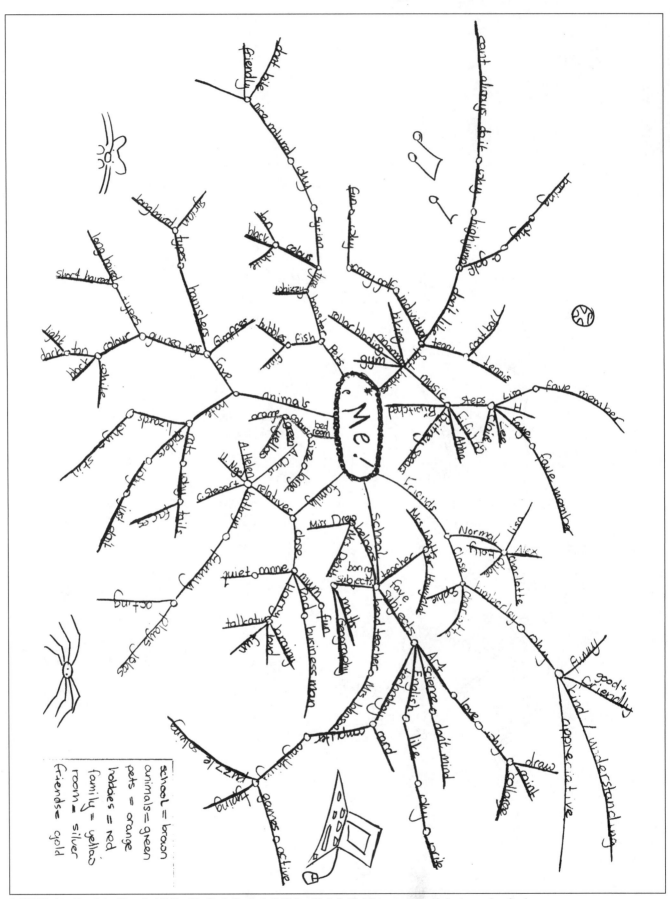

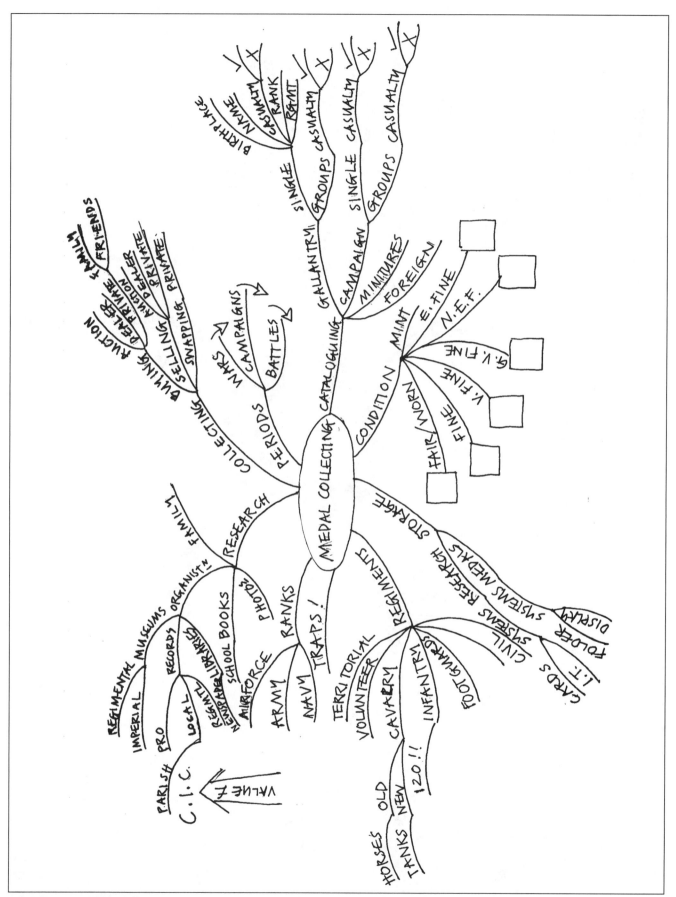

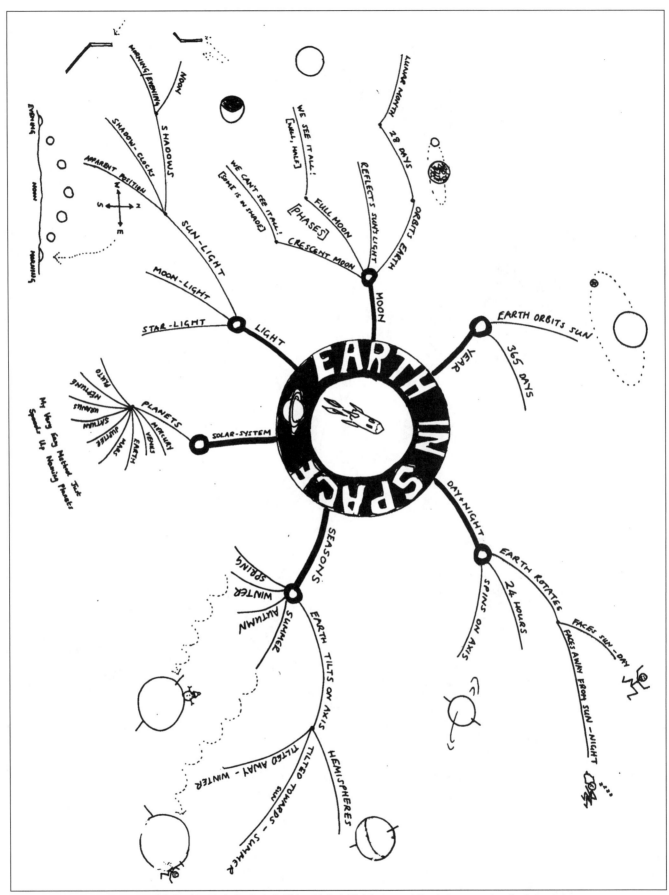

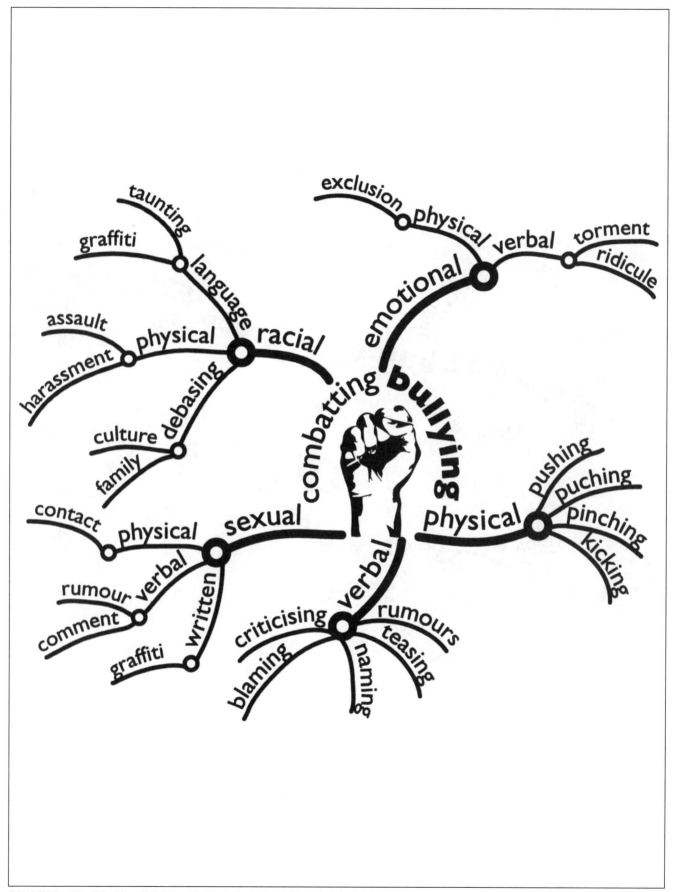

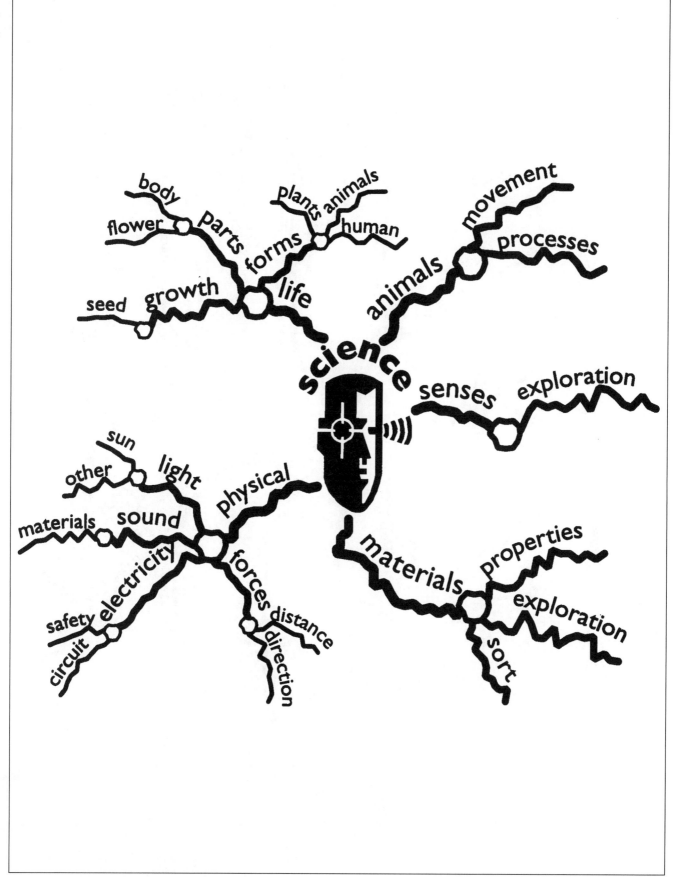

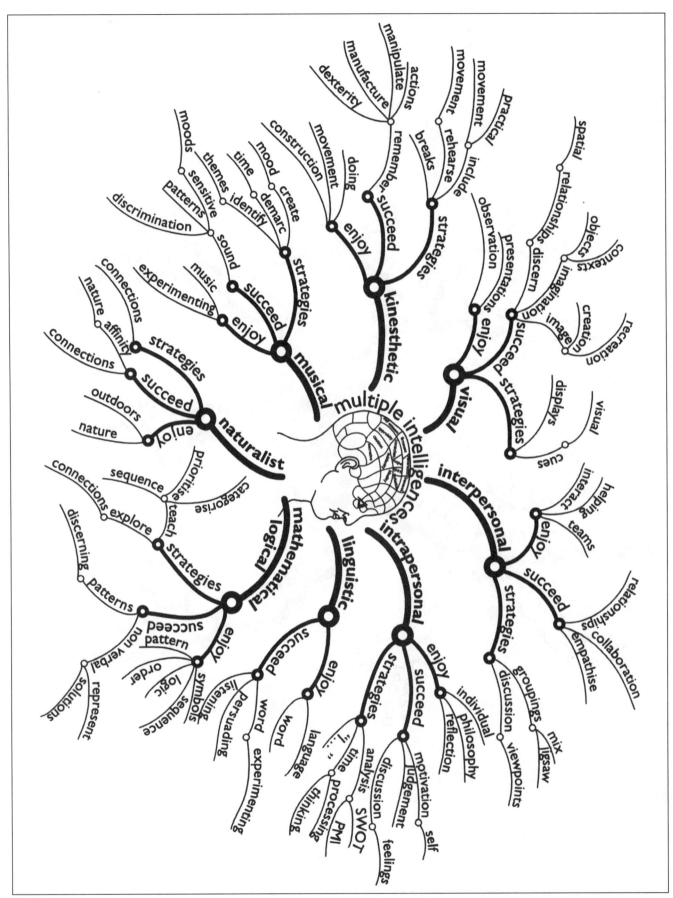

MIND MAPPING

METHODOLOGY

VISUALS
- WORDS
  - PRINT
    - KEY TYPE
      - NOUN — MOSTLY
      - VERB — SOME
      - ADJECTIVE — RARELY
- IMAGES
  - ICON
  - PICTURE
  - MEMORABLE

USES
- HOME
- SOCIAL
- SCHOOL
  - ACCELERATED LEARNING
  - PLAN
  - DO
  - REVIEW

ORDER
- CHUNK
  - 7±2
- CLASSIFY
- FORMAT
  - FISHBONE
  - HAYFORK

BENEFITS
- FUN
- SPEED
- CREATIVITY
- ORGANIZATION
- CONFIDENCE
- MEMORY
- COMMUNICATION
- INTEREST
- CONCENTRATION
- BRAIN FRIENDLY

References & Acknowledgments

Alder, H. and Heather, B. (1998). *NLP in 21 days*, Piatkus, London.

Avgerinou, M. and Ericson, J. (1997). "A Review of the Concept of Visual Literacy", *British Journal of Educational Technology* Vol. 28, No. 4, Oct. 1997, pp. 280–291.

Bannister, P. (1985). *Issues and Approaches in Personal Construct Theory*, Academic Press, London.

Blagg, N. (1991). *Can We Teach Intelligence?*, Lawrence Erlbaum, New York.

Blunkett, D. Minister for Education, speaking before addressing North of England Education Conference, 5 January 2000, quoted in *Daily Express* 6 January 2000.

Bower, G. H., Clark, M. C., Lesgold, A. M. and Winzenz, D. (1969). "Hierarchical Retrieval Schemes in Recall of Categorised Word Lists", in *Journal of Verbal Learning Language and Verbal Behaviour*, 8, pp. 323–43.

Britton, J. (1970). *Language and Learning*. Pelican, London [reproduced by permission of Penguin Books Ltd.]

Sherwood, D. (1988). *Unlock Your Mind*, Gower, Aldershot.

Bruner, J. S. (1971). *Towards a theory of instruction*, Oxford University Press, Oxford.

Bruer, J.T. (1997). "Education and the Brain: A Bridge Too Far," Educational Researcher, Vol. 26, No. 8, Nov. 1997 [copyright (1997) by the American Educational Research Association reproduced with permission of the publishers.]

Bruner, J. (1960). *Process of Education*, Vintage Books, New York, USA.

Buzan, T. (1993). *The Mindmap Book*, BBC, London.

Carter, R. (1999). *Mapping the Mind*, Cassell & Co., London.

Davis, W. S. and McCormack, A. (1979). *The Information Age*. Addison-Wesley, Reading, MA.

Dryden, G. and Vos. J. (1994). *The Learning Revolution*, Accelerated Learning Systems Ltd., Aylesbury.

Fisher, R. (1995). *Teaching Children to Learn*, Stanley Thornes, Cheltenham [reproduced with the permission of Stanley Thornes Publishers Ltd.].

Foster, G., Sowicki E., Schaeffer H., Zelinski V. (2002). *I Think, Therefore I Learn!*, Pembroke Publishers, Markham.

Foster, G. (1996). *Student Self-Assessment*, Pembroke Publishers, Markham.

Goleman, D. (1985). *Vital Lies, Simple Truths*, Bloomsbury, London.

Haber, R. N. (1970). "How We Remember What We See", *Scientific American*, 105, May 1970.

Heinich, R., Molenda, M., Russell, J. D. and Smaldino, S. E., (1996). *Instructional Media and Technologies for Learning – 5th edition*, Prentice-Hall, Englewood Cliffs, New Jersey.

Henderson, P. (1993). *How to Succeed in Examinations and Assessments – National Extension College*, Collins Educational, London.

Hughes, M. (1999). *Closing the Learning Gap*, Network Educational Press, Stafford.

Jensen, E. (1995). *Super Teaching*, The Brain Store Inc., USA.

Katz, L. G. (September 1993). "Dispositions as Educational Goals", *ERIC DIGEST*, University of Illinois.

Keates, J. S. (1982). *Understanding Maps*, Longman, Harlow.

Kelly, G. A. (1963). *A Theory of Personality*, Norton, New York [copyright © 1955, 1963 by George A. Kelly, renewed 1983, 1991 by Gladys Kelly, reprinted by permission of WW Norton & Co].

Kerry, T. (1998). *Questioning and Explaining in Classrooms*, Hodder and Stoughton, London.

Lewin, J. R., Schriberg, L. K. and Berry J. K. (1983). "A Concrete Strategy for Remembering Abstract Prose", American Educational Research Journal, Vol. 20, pp. 277–290 [copyright (1983) by the American Educational Research Association reproduced with permission from the publishers]

Long, S. A., Winograd, P. N. and Bridge, C. A. (1989). "The Effects of Reader and Text Characteristics and Imagery Repeated During and After Reading", *Reading Research Quarterly*, Vol. 24, No. 3, pp. 313–372.

Novak, J. D. (1998). *Learning, Creating and Using Knowledge*, Lawrence Erlbaum, New York, USA.

Marshall, S. P. (1995). *Schemas in Problem Solving*, Cambridge University Press, Cambridge.

Novak, J. D. and Gowin, D. B. (1984). *Learning How to Learn*, Cambridge University Press, Cambridge.

Miller, P. (1998). *Mobilising the Power of What You Know*, Random House, London.

McGuiness, C. (1999) . "From thinking skills to thinking schools", report for DfEE.

McPeck, J. E. (1990). *Teaching Critical Thinking*, Routledge, London.

O'Connor, J. and McDermott, I. (1997). *The Art of Systems Thinking*. Thorsons, California, USA.

Perkins, D. N. (1987). "Thinking Frames: An Integrating Perspective on Teaching Cognitive Skills", in Baron, J. and Sternberg, R. (1987). *Teaching Thinking Skills: Theory and Research*, W. H. Freeman, New York.

Postman, N. (1990). *Teaching as a Conserving Activity*, Delacorte, New York, USA.

Quin, P. (1987). "The Categorical Representations of Visual Pattern Information by Young Infants", *Cognition* 27, 145–179.

Riding, R. and Rayner, S. (1998). *Cognitive Styles and Learning Styles*, David Fulton, London.

Robbins, A. (1988). *Unlimited Power*, Simon and Schuster, London.

Rose, C. and Nicholl, M. J. (1997). *Accelerated Learning for the 21st Century*, Dell, New York.

Rumelhart, D. E. (1980). "Schemata: The Building Bricks of Cognition", in Spiro, R. J., Bruce, . C. and Brewer, W. F. (eds), *Theoretical Issues in Reading Comprehension*, Lawrence Erlbaum, New York, USA.

Senge, P. (1994). *Fifth Discipline Fieldbook*, Nicholas Brearley, London.

Schon, D. (1991). *The Reflective Practitioner*, Arena, Aldershot.

Schooler, J. (1998) in Claxton, G. *Hare Brain, Tortoise Mind*, Fourth Estate, London [reprinted by permission of Fourth Estate Ltd., copyright © (1997) Guy Claxton]

Schwab, J. J. (1970). "Structures of the disciplines: Meanings and Slogans", in Snook, I.A. (1970). "The Concept of Indoctrination", *Studies in Philosophy and Education*, Vol. 7, No. 2, Fall 1970.

Smith, A. and Call, N., (1999). *Accelerated Learning in Primary Schools*, Network Educational Press, Stafford.

Smothermon, R. (1980). *Winning Through Enlightenment*, Context, San Francisco.

Sternberg, R. J. (1997). *Thinking Styles*, Cambridge University Press, Cambridge.

Svantesson, I. (1998). *Learning Maps and Memory Skills*, Kogan Page, London.

Van Nagel, C., Reese, E. J., Reese, M. and Siudzinski, R. (1985). *Mega Teaching and Learning*, Metamorphous Press, Portland, Oregon USA.

Wenger, W. (1980) . *The Einstein Factor*, Prima, California, USA.

Woditsch, G. A. (1991). *The Thoughtful Teacher's Guide to Thinking Skills*, Lawrence Erlbaum Association, London.

Wragg, E. C. and Brown, G. (1993). *Explaining*, Routledge, London.

Wurman, R. S. (1991). *Information Anxiety*, Pan. London.

Index